Reconciling
Free Trade,
Fair Trade,
and Interdependence

Reconciling Free Trade, Fair Trade, and Interdependence

The Rhetoric of Presidential Economic Leadership

Delia B. Conti

Praeger Series in Political Communication

Westport, Connecticut
London

Library of Congress Cataloging-in-Publication Data

Conti, Delia B., 1961–
   Reconciling free trade, fair trade, and interdependence : the
rhetoric of presidential economic leadership / Delia B. Conti.
      p.   cm.—(Praeger series in political communication, ISSN
1062–5623)
      ISBN 0–275–96109–5 (alk. paper)
      1. United States—Commercial policy—History.   2. Free trade—
United States—History.   3. Presidents—United States—Messages.
4. Communication in politics—United States—History.   I. Title.
II. Series.
   HF1455.C744   1998
   382′.3′0973—dc21   97–27925

British Library Cataloguing in Publication Data is available.

Library of Congress Catalog Card Number: 97–27925
ISBN: 0–275–96109–5
ISSN: 1062–5623

First published in 1998

Praeger Publishers, 88 Post Road West, Westport, CT 06881
An imprint of Greenwood Publishing Group, Inc.

Printed in the United States of America

The paper used in this book complies with the
Permanent Paper Standard issued by the National
Information Standards Organization (Z39.48–1984).

10 9 8 7 6 5 4 3 2 1

Copyright Acknowledgments

The author and the publisher gratefully acknowledge permission for use of the following material:

From *American Business and Public Policy* by Raymond Bauer, Ithiel de Sola Pool, and Lewis Anthony Dexter. Copyright 1972. Reprinted by permission of Aldine de Gruyter.

From *The Kennedy Round in American Trade Policy* by John W. Evans. Copyright © 1971 by the President and Fellows of Harvard College. Reprinted by permission of Harvard University Press.

From *Trade Agreements and the Kennedy Round* by Stanley D. Metzger. Copyright 1964. Reprinted by permission of Stanley D. Metzger.

From *Between Hope and History* by William J. Clinton. Copyright © 1996 by William Jefferson Clinton. Reprinted by permission of Times Books, a division of Random House, Inc.

From *Making Economic Policy in Congress* by Allen Schick. Copyright 1983. Reprinted with the permission of The American Enterprise Institute for Public Policy Research, Washington, D.C.

From Delia B. Conti, "President Reagan's Trade Rhetoric: Lessons for the 1990's." Permission granted by the Center for the Study of the Presidency, publisher of *Presidential Studies Quarterly*.

From Delia B. Conti, "President Bush Embraces a New World Order: Foreign Cooperation and Domestic Confrontation," in *Bush Conference Proceedings*, ed., William F. Levantrosser and Rosanna Perotti, Greenwood Publishing Group, forthcoming. Reprinted by permission of William F. Levantrosser.

Contents

Series Foreword

Those of us from the discipline of communication studies have long believed that communication is prior to all other fields of inquiry. In several other forums I have argued that the essence of politics is "talk" or human interaction.[1] Such interaction may be formal or informal, verbal or nonverbal, public or private, but it is always persuasive, forcing us consciously or subconsciously to interpret, to evaluate, and to act. Communication is the vehicle for human action.

From this perspective, it is not surprising that Aristotle recognized the natural kinship of politics and communication in his writings *Politics* and *Rhetoric*. In the former, he establishes that humans are "political beings [who] alone of the animals [are] furnished with the faculty of language."[2] And in the latter, he begins his systematic analysis of discourse by proclaiming that "rhetorical study, in its strict sense, is concerned with the modes of persuasion."[3] Thus, it was recognized over 2,300 years ago that politics and communication go hand in hand because they are essential parts of human nature.

Back in 1981, Dan Nimmo and Keith Sanders proclaimed that political communication was an emerging field.[4] Although its origin, as noted, dates back centuries, a "self-consciously cross-disciplinary" focus began in the late 1950s. Thousands of books and articles later, colleges and universities offer a variety of graduate and undergraduate coursework in the area in such diverse departments as communication, mass communication, journalism, political science, and sociology.[5] In Nimmo and Sanders' early assessment, the "key areas of inquiry" included rhetorical analysis, propaganda analysis, attitude change studies, voting studies, government and the news media, functional and systems analyses, technological changes, media technologies, campaign techniques, and research techniques.[6] In a survey of the state of the field in 1983, the same authors and Lynda Kaid found additional, more specific areas of concerns such as the presidency, political polls, public opinion, debates, and advertising to name a few.[7] Since the first study, they also noted a shift away from the rather strict behavioral approach.

A decade later, Dan Nimmo and David Swanson argued that "political communication has developed some identity as a more or less distinct domain of scholarly work."[8] The scope and concerns of the area have further expanded to include critical theories and cultural studies. While there is no precise definition, method, or disciplinary home of the area of inquiry, its primary domain is the role, processes, and effects of communication within the context of politics broadly defined.

In 1985, the editors of *Political Communication Yearbook: 1984* noted that "more things are happening in the study, teaching, and practice of political communication than can be captured within the space limitations of the relatively few publications available."[9] In addition, they argued that the backgrounds of "those involved in the field [are] so varied and pluralist in outlook and approach, . . . it [is] a mistake to adhere slavishly to say any set format in shaping the content."[10] And more recently, Nimmo and Swanson called for "ways of overcoming the unhappy consequences of fragmentation within a framework that respects, encourages, and benefits from diverse scholarly commitments, agendas, and approaches."[11]

In agreement with these assessments of the area and with gentle encouragement, Praeger established the Praeger Series in Political Communication. The series is open to all qualitative and quantitative methodologies as well as contemporary and historical studies. The key to characterizing the studies in the series is the focus on communication variables or activities within a political context or dimension. As of this writing, nearly forty volumes have been published, and there are numerous impressive works forthcoming. Scholars from the disciplines of communication, history, journalism, political science, and sociology have participated in the series.

I am, without shame or modesty, a fan of the series. the joy of serving as its editor is in participating in the dialogue of the field of political communication and in reading the contributors' works. I invite you to join me.

Robert E. Denton, Jr.

NOTES

1. See Robert E. Denton, Jr., *The Symbolic Dimensions of the American Presidency* (Prospect Heights, Ill.: Waveland Press, 1982); Robert E. Denton, Jr., and Gary Woodward, *Political Communication in America* (New York: Praeger, 1985; 2nd ed., 1990); Robert E. Denton, Jr., and Dan Han, *Presidential Communication* (New York: Praeger, 1986); and Robert E. Denton, Jr., *The Primetime Presidency of Ronald Reagan* (New York: Praeger, 1988).

2. Aristotle, *The Politics of Aristotle*, trans. Ernest Barker (New York: Oxford University Press, 1970), p. 5.

3. Aristotle, *Rhetoric*, trans. Rhys Roberts (New York: The Modern Library, 1954), p. 22.

4. Dan Nimmo and Keith Sanders, "Introduction: The Emergence of Political Communication as a Field," in *Handbook of Political Communication*, eds. Dan Nimmo and Keith Sanders (Beverly Hills, Calif.: Sage, 1981), pp. 11–36.

5. Ibid., p. 15.

6. Ibid., pp. 17–27.

7. Keith Sanders, Lynda Kaid, and Dan Nimmo, eds., *Political Communication Yearbook: 1984* (Carbondale: Southern Illinois University, 1985), pp. 283–308.

8. Dan Nimmo and David Swanson, "The Field of Political Communication: Beyond the Voter Persuasion Paradigm," in *New Dimensions in Political Communication*, eds. David Swanson and Dan Nimmo (Beverly Hills, Calif.: Sage, 1990), p. 8.

9. Sanders, Kaid, and Nimmo, eds., *Political Communication Yearbook: 1984*, p. xiv.

10. Ibid.

11. Nimmo and Swanson, "The Field of Political Communication," p. 11.

Preface

Trade policy is an area where presidents have maintained a remarkably consistent rhetoric and a semblance of policy congruity throughout U.S. history. Presidents—from the founding fathers to contemporary executives—have uniformly espoused adherence to the principle of free trade. This has occurred despite vast changes in the economic status of the country and the institutional hierarchy of the presidency. The United States has evolved from a new nation of infant industries, to an economic powerhouse, and, today, an international leader in a world of increasing economic interdependence. The presidency has grown into an office of unparalleled power, which is nonetheless intricately restrained by the congressional and judicial branches as well as by a new institutional entity unforeseen by the writers of the Constitution—the broadcast media. The media, and in particular television, have fundamentally transformed the nature of the presidential office. The president's rhetorical powers now are the foundation of the executive's constitutional and legislative powers.[1] Presidents have gained immense power through their unmatched potential for persuasion, although they are equally challenged by new constraints in the form of intense public examination of their records and demands for consistency.

These fundamental changes in the nature of the executive office and the persuasive possibilities for the president have coincided with an increased need for presidential leadership in trade policy. Trade has evolved from the means through which the country gained revenues via tariffs to a primarily foreign policy issue under essentially executive control and, today, a domes-

tic issue resonating with the issues of economic nationalism and isolationism in reaction to an increasingly interdependent world.

What is most interesting about the changes in the rhetorical powers of
the presidential office and the evolving nature of trade policy is the distinct
nature of scholarship in political science and rhetoric. Political scientists
examine the powers of the presidency in the realms of foreign and domestic
policy, and rhetorical scholars examine the fundamental distinctions between presidential powers in the same realms. It is the political scientists,
however, who have studied the intersection of the foreign and domestic
policy areas in the realm of intermestic issues. Rhetorical scholars have yet
to analyze the rhetoric of intermestic issues, of which trade is the most
classic.

Thus, in this book I examine the rhetoric of trade policy and the implications for the rhetoric of intermestic issues. As trade policy has evolved to
match economic and political demands, the relative importance of foreign
and domestic policy concerns has, accordingly, shifted. The president must
balance personal preferences in trade—and remember, the contemporary
presidency has been consistently free trade–oriented—with the public's
clamor for interdependence or isolationism; for the expansion of free trade,
the fight for fair trade, or the retreat to economic isolationism.

The introduction establishes the work's rhetorical perspective. My analysis is based on an assessment of the president's rhetorical powers and of
their resulting influence on, and interplay with, his constitutional and
legislative powers. The first chapter provides a historical overview of
presidential arguments on trade, from its constitutional foundations to the
1930s revolution in trade policy, in which the focus of trade changed from
a domestic policy emphasis to a foreign policy issue. The second chapter
examines trade in the Cold War era with a focus on its use as a tool in the
fight to expand capitalism and democracy and to control and contain
communism. The remaining chapters focus on individual presidents and
their trade policy and rhetoric in the post–Cold War era. The third chapter
provides an assessment of President Ronald Reagan's trade rhetoric. Governing in an era of increasing economic interdependence, Reagan adhered
to a rigid free trade rhetoric despite making dramatic reversals on trade
policy; most notably, with devaluation of the dollar. The fourth chapter
assesses President George Bush's trade rhetoric. Bush largely continued in
the tradition of the Reagan presidency by espousing a free trade rhetoric
and a limited government—and thus remaining true to the Republican ideal
as well as the constraints of the budget deficit. However, President Bush
faced a revolution in international politics as he held office during the end

of the Cold War. Bush had to balance the use of trade as a foreign policy tool with domestic unease over an increasing trade deficit. Significantly, during Bush's administration, the bulk of the work occurred on the North American Free Trade Agreement (NAFTA) and the General Agreement on Tariffs and Trade (GATT) treaties. The fifth chapter examines the trade rhetoric of the Bill Clinton administration. President Clinton, while bene- fiting from (as well as working for) the passage of NAFTA and GATT, took a distinctly different tack from President Bush on trade policy. While continuing to espouse free trade, Clinton emphasized the domestic side of the equation and an enhanced role for government. The conclusion of this work presents rhetorical strategies for presidents regarding trade and other intermestic issues. In particular, future presidents would do well to prioritize domestic issues, maintain consistency, emphasize institutional legitimacy, and promote economic competitiveness.

NOTE

1. Theodore Windt, "Presidential Rhetoric: Definition of a Discipline of Study," in *Essays in Presidential Rhetoric*, ed. Theodore Windt and Beth Ingold, 2nd ed. (Dubuque, IA: Kendall/Hunt Publishing Company, 1987), xix–xxi.

Acknowledgments

I would like to thank Professor Theodore Windt for his early guidance on the rhetoric of trade policy and intermestic issues. I would also like to thank Professor Morris Ogul for his contributions and advice.

This volume would not have been possible without the support and encouragement of my family. Thus, I dedicate this book to my husband, Tony, and to my children, Sara, Anthony, and Alexandria.

Introduction

Despite vast disparities in governing philosophy and strategy, Presidents Reagan, Bush, and Clinton had at least one political goal in common: successful passage of the North American Free Trade Agreement (NAFTA). In fact, President Clinton was the benefactor of his Republican predecessors' efforts, for the NAFTA victory during his first term was hailed as a landmark success of the administration: a model of bipartisan support, and a triumph for the expansion of global commerce and continued free trade. However, Clinton did not trumpet this achievement in his reelection efforts. Moreover, the administration's decision to support NAFTA involved a last-minute resolution, a short public battle, and a narrow win. Examining the history of trade policy helps to clarify the ironies in this latest presidential battle. With the increasing importance of economic competitiveness, it is imperative for presidents to develop a clearer rhetorical strategy on trade, as well as other intermestic issues.

Trade policy has historically been a rhetorical landmine for presidents. The executive branch has adhered to the principle of free trade, while the public has supported protectionism. The legislative branch has further confounded the issue by inflaming protectionist pressures while passing the burden of action to the president. Presidents have responded by establishing quotas in the name of fair trade, thereby rhetorically preserving the principle of free trade.

Even with these vast changes in the substance of trade policy, presidential rhetoric on trade has remained relatively stable. Trade, as regulated through tariffs, has evolved from an accepted principle of international relations, a domestic source of revenue, and a tool for encouraging domestic industries to a controversial means through which to punish political enemies and reward political allies. Presidents continue to quietly protect politically powerful interests despite rhetorical devotion to the principle of free trade. They are able to do so, and they remain consistent in their rhetoric, through argument from definition: arguing that free trade entails the principle of reciprocity, they therefore practice it under the guise of fair trade.

President Reagan was the first contemporary president to be faced with an increasing trade deficit, heightened economic interdependence, and problematic domestic competitiveness. While he was especially adept at reconciling fair trade policy with a free trade rhetoric, his failure to deal constructively with the U.S. role in the changing international economic arena contributed to a massive trade deficit. Post–Cold War presidents have inherited the burden of reducing the deficit while establishing a new role for U.S. leadership in the realm of economic competition. The leadership of Presidents Reagan, Bush, and Clinton in the economic arena is the focus of this book. Their failures and successes provide lessons for future presidents' rhetoric on intermestic issues.

In this new era of economic competition and increasing interdependence, presidents can no longer rely on the public's inattention to trade policy. As the development of international institutions causes U.S. trade policy to evolve, a new rhetorical strategy must evolve as well.

THE RHETORICAL PERSPECTIVE OF THIS VOLUME

The scholarly literature pertinent to trade rhetoric rests in three academic disciplines: rhetorical criticism, political science, and economics. The focus of this analysis is rhetorical criticism—more particularly, presidential rhetoric. Theodore Windt divides presidential power into three areas: constitutional or legal power, power derived from the president's role as legislative leader and head of the party, and power derived from public opinion.[1]

Constitutional power encompasses power granted by the Constitution and that conferred by law. In trade, the Constitution grants power to Congress for regulating commerce. The president retains the right to engage in negotiations with foreign nations to establish treaties, with the advice and consent of the Senate. Congress, though, has delegated control over trade to the executive. The president must act within the parameters of acceptable action as defined by Congress; thus, establishing trade policy becomes a delicate balancing act of accommodating foreign nations while responding to congressional pressures. As chief executive, the president also holds the power of providing for the national defense, and indeed, presidents have justified actions in trade policy on the grounds of establishing and maintaining basic defense-related manufacturers. Also relevant to the president's powers as chief executive is control over the the executive branch bureaucracy. There are several departments that regulate trade, including Commerce, Defense, and State. The Office of the Special Trade Representative was established as part of the Trade Expansion Act of 1962 for the express purpose of coordinating trade policy. Nevertheless, bureaucratic infighting over priorities controlling trade policy has been a consistent problem for the executive, with the predominant conflict involving competing foreign and domestic political concerns.

The second source of presidential power is power derived from the president's role as party, or legislative, leader. The ability of the president to persuade Congress is especially crucial in trade policy, as the latter can shape the political atmospherics for the administration. Congress retains the right to constrict or expand the president's power through legislation. This legislative "dance" is a prime influence on trade and establishes the environment in which an administration sets policy. Congress often introduces bills proposing protectionist legislation, which serve as signals to the executive to act on trade. This proposed legislation creates political opportunities for the president by providing tools with which the executive can attempt to pry open foreign markets to U.S. exports.[2] House and Senate votes are often scheduled prior to international economic summits or concurrent with presidential meetings with foreign heads of state.

The third source of presidential power is the power derived from public opinion—which is the foundation of the president's constitutional and legislative powers: "It is the power upon which all other powers rest, for persuasion is how public opinion is formed, changed, influenced, and molded."[3] Rhetorical critics study the public statements of presidents: speeches, news conferences, and messages to Congress. They also study target constituencies and the uses of the mass media.[4] However, due to the volatility of public opinion on trade, presidents rarely appeal directly to the populace. This in itself is a significant rhetorical choice. However, avoiding major speeches as a platform is not equivalent to ignoring the rhetorical opportunities relevant to trade policy. The president can be portrayed as an active leader through visual presentations at international economic summits while simultaneously promoting the image of domestic economic strength through visual presentations at American manufacturing plants. As the presidency has undergone the transformation from a "constitutional, administrative office to an executive, rhetorical office,"[5] the rhetorical strategies on trade have undergone a similar evolution.[6]

According to Ceaser, Thurow, Tulis, and Bessette's "The Rise of the Rhetorical Presidency," the presidential office has changed for three reasons: a new, activist leadership by modern presidents; advances in communication technologies; and the modern mass media.[7] Presidents traditionally have found it to their advantage to keep trade off the public agenda. Making it an issue activates the inherently protectionist public, thus disadvantaging the free trade–oriented executive. However, keeping trade off the public agenda does not translate into ignoring the persuasive possibilities of television—especially the network news. Thus, even with the newfound power of the rhetorical presidency, the instability of public opinion on trade often works to the president's disadvantage, and consequently, the rhetorical power of the executive office is left unplumbed.

The characteristics of trade as an intermestic issue directly results in this volatility, as presidents must balance foreign policy interests with domestic concerns. Two articles that provide relevant insight into the nature of the rhetoric of trade policy are Philip Wander's "The Rhetoric of American Foreign Policy" and Ryan J. Barilleaux's "The President, 'Intermestic Issues,' and the Risks of Policy Leadership."[8] Wander's article highlights the dualities and polarizations characteristic of presidential trade rhetoric, which Wander labels "prophetic dualism":

In its perfected form prophetic dualism divides the world into two camps. Between them there is conflict. One side acts in accord with all that is good, decent, and at one with God's will. The other acts in direct opposition. Conflict between them is resolved only through the total victory of one side over the other. Since no guarantee exists that good will triumph, there is no middle ground. Hence neutrality may be treated as delusion, compromise appeasement, and negotiation a call for surrender.[9]

The defining feature of the Cold War was the dualism of the United States versus the Soviet Union. Replacing this set, although not of equal force, is the dualism of democracy versus totalitarianism. In trade, the characteristic dualism is that of free trade versus protectionism. The economic nationalism characteristic of trade rhetoric illustrates the "religious cast to public discourse" inherent in prophetic dualism, in which "piety becomes especially thick about the 'nation.' "[10] Economic nationalism has become a more potent force as economic competition has replaced military competition, resulting in what Wander defined as "technocratic realism."[11] The foreign policy influences on trade rhetoric introduce political considerations into what is theoretically an essentially economic equation. In this nationalist rhetoric, nations do not merely violate economic ideals, they act aggressively, threatening American economic interests. "The rhetoric of American foreign policy has to do with nations. Nations, in official statements, are personified. They act morally and immorally. They use force. They violate one another's rights."[12]

It is this intersection of foreign and domestic policy that leads Barilleaux to define trade policy as the paradigmatic intermestic issue. "In many ways, trade is the classic intermestic issue: it is about the American economy as it interacts with the rest of the world."[13] Barilleaux defines intermestic issues as "those matters of international relations which, by their very nature, closely involve the domestic economy of a nation."[14] He further argues that the risks of leadership in intermestic affairs are greater than for other foreign policy issues because in intermestic affairs, the president has to consider domestic actors in the political context, especially Congress and the pressure of public opinion. Herein lies the major challenge for presidential rhetoric on trade. The president must persuade foreign nations that he is truly trying to preserve free trade through open markets while convincing domestic actors that he is pushing for fair trade and acting to protect American interests as necessary.

Because trade is an intermestic issue and because foreign and domestic policy interests overlap, there exists a conundrum in trade policy. The executive, as foreign policy leader, has consistently favored free trade. The members of the legislative branch, speaking for their constituencies, have consistently favored protectionism—at least in the postwar years, when this was reflective of public opinion. However, the executive is also beholden to domestic constituencies and therefore must balance foreign and domestic interests. The president, in his rhetoric, must uphold the principle of free trade in the interests of the international marketplace—while protecting the nation's economic interests, which are apparently better served by protectionism. While this particular dilemma has been consistently present throughout the history of the United States, current economic conditions have elevated this political and rhetorical problem to new heights. The pervasiveness of the media—especially the growing importance of television—has heightened the president's dilemma of reconciling foreign and domestic interests in trade policy.[15]

THE ORGANIZATION OF THIS STUDY

Because the United States is grounded in democratic capitalism, it is not surprising that a free trade rhetoric based on Adam Smith has remained the theoretical foundation for trade policy. However, the economic theory of pure free trade has never been perfectly applied in U.S. trade policy. From the use of tariffs as a source of revenue to their use for political support, placing restrictions on imports is an accepted facet of trade policy. Presidential rhetoric on trade has remained consistent in its arguments: trade should be reciprocal, and thus fair; it should be restricted to protect domestic industries; and trade policy can be used to reinforce political alliances. What has changed is the emphasis accorded such arguments. However, the defense of the principle of free trade has remained an executive constant.

Thus, this volume begins with an examination of the history of trade policy and rhetoric. First is an assessment of the constitutional foundations of trade policy, a look at sectional divisions preceding the Civil War, and a discussion of trade policy at the turn of the nineteenth century, in the 1930s, after World War II, and in the 1970s. Each time span marked a significant period and change in trade policy. In these years, the United States grew from an infant economy to an economic superpower, and trade policy was integral to this growth. What has marked it in contemporary times is erosion of this economic power. While the United States remains the leading nation militarily and a strong nation economically, the growing trade deficit and increasingly blurred boundaries of international investment have dramatically changed the boundaries for trade policy and rhetoric.

Thus, contemporary presidents have to negotiate both the unique (and increasingly difficult to balance) constraints in trade policy and the new demands of the rhetorical presidency. Presidents Reagan, Bush, and Clinton are the focus of the remainder of this work. A separate chapter assesses the policy constraints, partisan preferences, and rhetorical strategies of each president in trade policy. Their rhetorical successes, failures, and difficulties in balancing the new demands of trade rhetoric can suggest strategies for future presidents when dealing with intermestic issues.

NOTES

1. Theodore Windt, "Presidential Rhetoric: Definition of a Discipline of Study," in *Essays in Presidential Rhetoric*, ed. Theodore Windt and Beth Ingold, 2nd ed. (Dubuque, IA: Kendall/Hunt Publishing Company, 1987), xix–xxi.

2. For an explanation of the "cry-and-sigh" syndrome, see Robert A. Pastor, *Congress and the Politics of U.S. Foreign Economic Policy 1929–1976* (Berkeley: University of California Press, 1980).

3. Windt, xxi.

4. Ibid.

5. Ibid., xxii.

6. See James W. Ceaser, Glenn E. Thurow, Jeffrey Tulis, and Joseph M. Bessette, "The Rise of the Rhetorical Presidency," *Presidential Studies Quarterly*, 11, no. 2 (Spring 1981): 158–171.

7. Ibid.

8. Philip Wander, "The Rhetoric of American Foreign Policy," *Quarterly Journal of Speech*, 70, no. 4 (November 1984): 339–361; Ryan J. Barilleaux, "The President, 'Intermestic Issues,' and the Risks of Policy Leadership," *Presidential Studies Quarterly*, 15, no. 4 (Fall 1985): 754–767.

9. Wander, 342.

10. Ibid., 343.

11. Ibid., 349.

12. Ibid., 353.

13. Barilleaux, 754–755.

14. Ibid.

15. For an assessment of the growing influence of the media on the rhetorical presidency, see Windt, "Presidential Rhetoric," and Ceaser, Thurow, Tulis, and Bessette, "Rise of the Rhetorical Presidency."

Chapter One

Presidential Rhetoric on Trade: A Historical Overview

There are six distinct periods in the development of the rhetoric of trade policy: first, establishing the constitutional foundations of trade; second, sectional divisions prior to the Civil War; third, populism in the 1880s, as embodied by a fight against tariffs; fourth, a revolution in trade policy during the 1930s; fifth, economic dominance following World War II; and sixth, the devaluation of the dollar and rising protectionist pressures in the 1970s and the 1980s. In each period, certain presidential trade arguments dominated. In some points, the fundamental principles of trade policy and the use of tariffs as an instrument of this policy were at issue. However, the executive branch remained unwavering in its public commitment to the principle of free trade. Even ardently protectionist presidents enveloped their trade-restricting actions in the cloak of reciprocity, defining such measures as necessitated by other nations' transgressions, and thereby rhetorically preserving their adherence to the principle of free trade. For Democrat and Republican presidents alike, adherence to free trade was essential in the land of Adam Smith and the free market. While each president had to balance government action with his own party's philosophy and the unique historical circumstances of the time, all rooted their trade rhetoric in the governing principles established in the U.S. Constitution.

THE CONSTITUTIONAL FOUNDATIONS OF TRADE

The Constitution gave a clear prerogative to Congress for regulating trade with foreign nations:

Article 1, Section 8: The Congress shall have power to lay and collect taxes, duties, imposts, and excises; to pay the debts and provide for the common defence and general welfare of the United States: but all duties, imposts, and excises, shall be uniform throughout the United States. . . . The Congress shall have power to regulate commerce with foreign nations.

Indeed, difficulty in setting a consistent policy on trade was one rationale for rewriting the Articles of Confederation.[1] The nation's experiences under the Articles of Confederation strengthened support for the principle of free trade, which was premised on the existence of equal terms of trade with other nations. An indication of the general acceptance of the need for a federal trade policy was the lack of convention debate over the relevant constitutional provisions. In the fourth Federalist Paper, John Jay recognized the inherent nationalism of trade policy:

The extension of our own commerce in our own vessels cannot give pleasure to any nations who possess territories on or near this continent, because the cheapness and excellence of our productions, added to the circumstance of vicinity, and the enterprise and address of our merchants and navigators, will give us a greater share in the advantages which those territories afford, than consists with the wishes or policy of their respective sovereigns.[2]

However, what was distinct about the tariff in the eighteenth and nineteenth centuries was its use as the primary means of revenue for the nation, protecting infant industries was a subordinate issue. The tariff was seen as necessary to preserve a strong union: by ensuring income and protecting free trade based on the principle of reciprocity.

The Tariff of 1789: The Principle of Reciprocity

John Adams, Thomas Jefferson, Ben Franklin, James Madison, and Patrick Henry all favored free trade in theory. They also believed (with the exception of Franklin) in the principle of reciprocity: that foreign restrictions on trade should be met with like restrictions on the part of the United States. Alexander Hamilton alone stood for the principle of protectionism to the exclusion of free trade.[3] Adams stated: "The United States must repel monopolies by monopolies and answer prohibitions by prohibitions."[4] Free trade buttressed by the principle of reciprocity was embodied in the Tariff of 1789.

The Tariff of 1789 imposed a tariff of less than 8 percent ad valorem on imports. The tariff was intended to be "protective in intention and spirit" by raising revenue, promoting infant industries, and ensuring reciprocity.[5] President George Washington, in his first annual address, advocated restrictions on trade in order to promote economic and political independence. Protecting domestic manufacturers was essential to the nation's defense: "A free people ought not only to be armed but disciplined; to which end a uniform and well-digested plan is requisite; and their safety and interest require that they should promote such manufactories as tend to render them independent of others for essential, particularly military, supplies."[6]

In summary, by 1789, the first year of the republic, the traditional executive arguments supporting free trade had been established. Limited protection was acceptable for three purposes: to fight unfair trade, to establish and protect infant industries, and to provide for basic manufacturers necessary for the national defense. These arguments were codified in Hamilton's 1791 *Report on Manufacturers*.

Hamilton's *Report on Manufacturers*

The *Report on Manufacturers* was prepared by the secretary of the treasury at a congressional request in reply to Washington's call for limited protection. The report established the utility of protection and specified the process of selecting protected items. Hamilton's brief remains a thorough examination of the economic and constitutional arguments in favor of protection. He argued that the need to encourage domestic manufacturers was widely accepted as ensuring the growth of infant industries and providing the manufactures necessary for the national defense. He agreed with the principle of free trade in theory while supporting the practice of fair trade as necessitated by the actions of foreign nations.

Throughout the history of trade policy, the argument of protecting one segment of the populace to the detriment of others has been central. Theoretically, the entire citizenry would benefit from free trade by enjoying lower prices on imported items regardless of the practices of foreign nations. However, in reality these benefits are widespread and diffuse. It is far easier to assess the damages to specific constituencies from unfair trading practices. One traditional divide has involved agricultural versus manufacturing interests. In Hamilton's day, the argument was a fundamental question of lifestyle; manufacturing had not yet come to dominate the American landscape. Hamilton argued that manufacturing and agriculture complemented each other. Manufacturers provided employment to agricultural laborers during downtimes, while agriculture benefited from the increased demand from consumers employed in manufacturing. While the specific rationale has changed from involving the general characteristic of the nation to the export of agricultural products versus the restriction of manufactured imports, the regional battle between urban and rural interests continues.

Essential to the infant industry argument was the temporary nature of tariffs, which are deemed necessary to reconciling protectionist actions with the ideal of free trade. It was in this temporary nature of tariffs that economic theory would clash with political reality. In theory, tariffs would be removed. While Hamilton was discussing the reluctance of the new nation to shift from an agrarian to a manufacturing society, his recognition of the need for leadership applies equally to the need to resist vocal protectionist forces against the broader national interest:

Experience teaches that men are often so much governed by what they are accustomed to see and practice, that the simplest and most obvious improvements in the most ordinary occupations are adopted with hesitation, reluctance, and by slow gradations. The spontaneous transition to new pursuits in a community long habituated to different ones may be expected to be attended with proportionately greater difficulty. . . . To produce the desirable changes as early as may be expedient may, therefore, require the incitement and patronage of the government.[7]

Hamilton, who was associated with Eastern manufacturing, was indeed representing his own best interests. Nonetheless he was prescient in recognizing the need for leadership, most suitably by the executive, in facilitating change in times of transition. It is much easier for presidents to reconcile protectionist actions with the ideal of free trade than to cling to a policy of free trade despite foreign transgressions. Presidents represent the national interest, and therefore they can define their actions, not as necessitated by particular interests, but rather as motivated by the need to defend America against the unfair actions of foreign nations:

Certain nations grant bounties on the exportation of particular commodities to enable their own workmen to undersell and supplant all competitors in the countries to which those commodities are sent. Hence the undertakers of a new manufacture have to contend not only with the natural disadvantages of a new undertaking, but with the gratuities and remunerations which other governments bestow. To be enabled to contend with success, it is evident that the interference and aid of their own governments are indispensable.[8]

In summary, in the first section of the *Report on Manufacturers*, Hamilton argued that government regulation of trade was necessary in order to promote a manufacturing base to establish infant industries, ensure national security, and protect manufacturers from predatory foreign nations. Having thus justified government intervention, Hamilton, in the second section of the report, specified the means by which to do so.

First, the United States should impose duties on foreign goods that competed with domestic infant industries. Second, the United States should enact prohibitions or establish equivalent duties on rival articles in order to "insure a due competition and an adequate supply on reasonable terms." These two measures were critical to establishing a domestic manufacturing base. Hamilton then suggested nine ancillary actions: first, prohibitions on the exportation of the materials of manufacturers—to be used sparingly; second, "pecuniary bounties," or grants of money, to new industries; third, premiums to award excellence; fourth, the exemption of the materials of manufacturers from duty; fifth, drawbacks of the duties previously imposed on the materials of manufacturers; sixth, the encouragement of new inventions and discoveries at home; seventh, judicious regulations for the inspection of manufactured commodities; eighth, the general circulation of bank paper; and ninth, internal improvements to facilitate the transportation of commodities.

Several of these measures remain integral to contemporary trade policy, especially those aimed at protecting and encouraging infant industries; imposing duties on rival articles—most often imposed for political (i.e., electoral) reasons; encouraging excellence and invention; making transportation improvements; and regulating monetary policy. Moreover, Hamilton's justification of economic intervention by the government was consistent with the emphasis of contemporary business executives on export promotion. When imports were restricted, the action was defined as justified by the ultimate aim of expanding trade through increased exports. While the arguments for and against protection would change in emphasis, the issues contained in Hamilton's 1791 *Report on Manufacturers* provided the political and rhetorical basis for trade policy throughout U.S. history.

The Perversion of the Infant Industries Argument

Although Hamilton's *Report on Manufacturers* powerfully advocated protectionism in the name of fair trade, the moderation in the Tariff of 1789 was maintained and may have served as the precedent for the later tendency of strong protectionist rhetoric to outstrip pragmatic policy initiatives. There was no change in policy because there was no surplus labor for new industries, manufacturers were not organized, there was a lack of foreign imports due to war, and political leaders failed to push for protection.[9]

Although duties did not increase, tariffs remained the primary source of revenue for the government. U.S. commerce flourished, in no small measure aided by European wars. Complications in 1808 with England and France marked a turning point in U.S. industrial history. During the War of 1812, foreign trade virtually ceased, which served as a stimulus to manufacturing and caused the danger of relying on foreign markets to become clear. The protection of infant industries remained a potent issue when trade resumed, as Britain flooded the U.S. market with surplus products from inventories swelled by the demands of the Napoleanic Wars. Despite high tariffs, many domestic industries suffered. Protectionist forces grew in strength and were able to link tariffs with anti-British sentiment and American nationalism.[10] As a consequence of the growth in anti-British sentiment and the rise in American manufacturing, restrictive legislation from 1808 to 1815 was "equivalent to extreme protection."[11] Protection had progressed from a temporary measure boosting American industry to a means of defending it, which became an accepted principle and practice.

Proponents of protection in the 1800s argued that the protection of infant industries had succeeded in lowering the prices of manufactured goods. A large measure of this fall in prices, however, was a result of improvements in manufacturing productivity, which illustrated the ease of fallacious argument in economics.

The repeated triumphant parading of a bare fall in prices as evidence of success in the working of protection is perhaps only a part of the general shallowness of the stock presentation of the protectionist case. Yet this sort of presentation is often made by earnest and intelligent men, convinced of the goodness of their case; one more instance, among many that are sadly familiar, to show that the most elementary economic propositions are little understood, and the simplest economic reasoning needs to be stated and illustrated again and again.[12]

The infant industries rationale for extending protection applied not only to establishing manufacturers, but also to alleviating economic hardships in times of transition: "There is scope for protection to young industries even in such a late stage of development. Any period of transition and of great industrial change may present the opportunity. . . . None the less the early stage of any new industry remains difficult. In every direction economists have come to recognize the immense force of custom and routine, even in countries where mobility and enterprise are at the highest."[13] The complexities of economic argument, combined with the difficulty of change in government policies—even in periods of transition—to make perversion of the infant industries argument relatively easy. While continued protection could be justified for reasons other than economic (e.g., political, social, or military), the tendency was for rhetoric to cling to outmoded economic justifications:

When customs duties have kept foreign competitors out of the market for twenty or thirty years; when a trade has habituated itself to domestic supply only; when there is a great din about pauper labor, designing foreigners, ruinous flooding of the market and what not, there will be opposition to the removal of duties, even though in fact the removal would make no difference. All business men, and all workmen likewise, are uneasy about intruders.[14]

In other words, advocates of protection could readily target foreign nations as scapegoats: "The special fear of the price-cutting foreigner doubtless reflects a protectionist feeling which goes far beyond the limits of the young industries argument, a feeling of suspicion and dislike against foreign supply at any time and under any conditions."[15] With this broadened rationale for the protection of infant industries, the argument itself changed in character: "Arguments used to justify protection changed from pleas for exceptional measures on behalf of infant industries to doctrines that made protection a right and a principle."[16] The infant industries argument, in the form of protecting established domestic manufacturers against foreign competition, remains a staple of contemporary trade rhetoric. It has retained its potency because it is a vehicle for transferred national sentiment.

THE YEARS 1820–1864: SECTIONAL DIVISIONS

President Monroe's Annual Messages of 1822 and 1823

Presidential messages in the 1800s reflected the changing points of contention in tariff policy. The perversion of the infant industry argument, as embodied by the elimination of the temporary basis for tariffs, was evident in President James Monroe's annual messages of 1822 and 1823. Monroe continued to present the free market as the ideal while in practice allowing protectionist measures in the guise of protecting the nation's national security and promoting economic independence. In his 1822 annual message, Monroe argued that these latter conditions preempted the free market ideal: "Satisfied I am, whatever may be the abstract doctrine in favor of unrestricted commerce, provided all nations would concur in it, and it was not liable to be interrupted by war, which has never occurred and cannot be expected, that there are other strong reasons applicable to our

situation and relations with other countries which impose on us the obligation to cherish and sustain our manufactures."[17]

Thus, Monroe advocated raising duties despite evidence that manufacturers were prospering under current levels. In his 1823 annual message,
Monroe urged continued protection in the name of national defense and
economic independence: "I recommend a review of the tariff for the purpose
of affording such additional protection to those articles which we are
prepared to manufacture, or which are more immediately connected with
the defence and independence of the country."[18] By the 1820s, the original
purpose of the tariff—providing revenue to the new country—had been
divorced from its continuance. Revenue remained an issue but had become
tangential in debates about the tariff: "It is true the fiscal effect of the
proposed act was referred to frequently in the debates, but on the one hand
the measure was condemned by its opponents as tending seriously to impair
the revenue, and on the other hand it was defended as not likely to result in
a diminution of receipts."[19] The tariff had become an accepted political
reality and was now used to protect American trade from foreign competition; yet as the use of tariffs spread, sectional divisions began to surface.

The South opposed the tariff as detrimental to the exportation of cotton.
Southerners thus argued that tariffs violated the Constitution by forbidding
duties on exports. In addition, Southerners argued that protective duties
constituted a tax on consumers to the benefit of particular classes, were
burdensome on agriculture, and promoted smuggling. Northerners countered that tariffs were necessary for maintaining home markets, relieving
the distress of manufacturers, and thereby promoting the solidarity of
agriculture, commerce, and manufacturing. These sectional divisions remain today, but they were heightened in the 1800s as the country began to
split apart prior to the Civil War. Tariffs were one issue indicative of this
regional tension and controversy over the rights and responsibilities of the
federal government.

President Jackson's Annual Messages of 1829, 1831, and 1832

Consistent with previous presidents, President Andrew Jackson adhered
to the principle of free trade tempered by reciprocity and allowing for the
provision of a strong manufacturing base as necessary for the national
defense: "The general rules to be applied in graduating the duties upon
articles of foreign growth or manufacture is that which will place our own
in fair competition with those of other countries; and the inducements to

advance even a step beyond this point are controlling in regard to those articles which are of prime necessity in case of war."[20] However, in this 1829 message, Jackson made explicit his presidential responsibility to protect the national interest in the face of sectional divisions. In addition, he argued that he remained true to the agricultural soul of the nation. Jackson maintained that ensuring a strong manufacturing base would in fact serve agricultural interests: "It is principally as manufactures and commerce tend to increase the value of agricultural productions and to extend their application to the wants and comforts of society that they deserve the fostering care of government."[21] However, by 1829, as the public debt diminished, the need for the tariff for increased revenue also declined and Jackson began to allow for the reduction and elimination of some tariffs—in this message, on tea and coffee.

More critically, though, a sign of the continued acceptance of the tariff beyond its original revenue-providing purpose was the attempt by Jackson to permanently institutionalize a means via which to provide for the disposal of excess funds resulting from tariffs: "He anticipated that the people would continue to insist upon a tariff that would yield far more revenue than was needed, in order to protect manufactures, and so far was he from regarding as unconstitutional a tariff for other purposes than revenue, that he advised a change in the Constitution to provide for the permanence of the policy by opening a sluiceway for the discharge of the excessive revenue."[22]

However, by 1831 sectional divisions were threatening the unity of the country and Jackson changed his emphasis from disposing of excess tariff revenue to reducing tariffs to the minimum levels necessary for revenue. "A modification of the tariff which shall produce a reduction of our revenue to the wants of the government and an adjustment of the duties on imports with a view to equal justice in relation to all our national interests and to the counteraction of foreign policy as far as it may be injurious to those interests, is deemed to be one of the principal objects which demand the consideration of the present Congress."[23]

Jackson now defined excess revenue as far from beneficial; indeed, it constituted unwarranted taxation: "It is therefore desirable that arrangements be adopted at your present session to relieve the people from unnecessary taxation after the extinguishment of the public debt."[24] President Jackson implored legislators to put the national interest above parochial concerns in this time of crisis: "In the exercise of that spirit of concession and conciliation which has distinguished the friends of our Union in all great emergencies, it is believed that this object may be effected without injury to any national interest."[25] Jackson argued that the benefits of encouraging domestic manufacturers did not outweigh the dangers of inflaming sectional divisions: "Experience makes it doubtful whether the advantages of this system are not counter-balanced by many evils, and whether it does not tend to beget in the minds of a large portion of our countrymen a spirit of discontent and jealousy dangerous to the stability of the Union."[26] Herein lay the critical distinction between Jackson's 1829 and 1831 annual messages. Jackson now reduced the legitimate purpose of the tariff to ensuring the national defense and would not accept continued protection as a political convenience: "Those who take an enlarged view of the condition of our country must be satisfied that the policy of protection must be ultimately limited to those articles of domestic manu- facture which are indispensable to our safety in time of war. Within this scope, on a reasonable scale, it is recommended by every consideration of patriotism and duty, which will doubtless always secure to it a liberal and efficient support."[27]

Economic decisions are infused with political considerations, which is precisely why tariffs continue to be enacted despite all economic protests to the contrary. In times of crisis and periods of transition, this conflict between economic ideals and political necessities reaches a stasis point and surfaces on the public agenda. By 1831, however, controversy over tariffs had been subordinated to the political dangers of southern secession.

The Compromise of 1833

Congress did not heed President Jackson's warnings against maintaining continued high tariffs for purposes other than revenue. The Tariff of 1832 thus contained high tariffs, and South Carolina threatened secession rather than submitting to them. In the subsequent legislative fight over the tariff, the argument for political protection as a necessary evil against foreign encroachment was not automatically assumed. The protectionists did not have the force of conviction of the threatened secessionists, nor any com- pelling rationale for maintaining high tariffs in the face of adequate revenue and established manufacturers.

From the first the protectionists realized that they had to fight for existence. They were confronted by a united and determined enemy, and were weakened for the contest by having among them many men who were timid, although loyal, and many more who were false and ready at the right moment for their own political future to desert to the other side. They were indignant while they were despondent. The bill seemed to them a needless and ruinous surrender of the protective system, which was not called for by any truly national interest. Its provisions were radical both as to the permanent rates of duty proposed and as to the suddenness with which the drop to those rates was to be made.[28]

In an attempt to save the Union, Senator Henry Clay (R–Ky.) introduced the Compromise Bill of 1833, which, while preserving the constitutional right to maintain protection, also set limits thereon:

The temper of Congress under the influence of the withdrawal of all pretense of support by the President, of the pressure by the Southern members and the subserviency of that class of Northern men aptly described by John Randolph as "doughfaces," and above all of the unanswerable argument that the Treasury did not need the high taxes, the temper of Congress in these circumstances was clearly in favor of a radical treatment of the tariff question. His purpose being to save what he could, Mr. Clay was surely right. His conduct was dictated by political consid-erations not less than was that of the free traders of the House. Undoubtedly he saved his cause from a crushing and overwhelming defeat.[29]

Clay's "Compromise of 1833," which limited tariffs to mostly revenue purposes, passed Congress. Thus the fight for preservation of the Union prevailed over northern support for tariffs.

THE 1880s: TRADE AND THE FIGHT AGAINST TARIFFS

President Grover Cleveland's Fight Against Excessive Tariffs

The 1880s were a period of transition. Tariffs were a necessary first step preceding more fundamental changes, most notably the elimination of trusts. In 1887, President Cleveland devoted his entire annual message to the subject of the tariff. He argued for a reduction of surplus revenues through a revision of the rate of duties on imports. In doing so, he echoed Jackson's 1831 and 1832 annual messages, even adhering to the definition of high tariffs as unwarranted taxation: "Our present tariff laws, the vicious, inequitable, and illogical source of unnecessary taxation, ought to be at once revised and amended."[30]

Cleveland accepted the assertion that duties remained necessary as a means of providing revenue: "It is not proposed to entirely relieve the country of this taxation. It must be extensively continued as the source of the government's income; and in a readjustment of our tariff the interests of American labor engaged in manufacture should be carefully considered, as well as the preservation of our manufacturers."[31]

Thus Cleveland allowed the use of tariffs for purposes other than providing revenue, most notably for protecting domestic manufacturers in the name of fair trade "because they render it possible for those of our people who are manufacturers to make these taxed articles and sell them for a price equal to that demanded for the imported goods that have paid customs duty."[32] What he did not abide was excessive tariffs promoted through the unwarranted use of the infant industries argument:

We are in the midst of centennial celebrations, and with becoming pride we rejoice in American skill and ingenuity, in American energy and enterprise, and in the wonderful natural advantages and resources developed by a century of national growth. Yet when an attempt is made to justify a scheme which permits a tax to be laid upon every consumer in the land for the benefit of our manufacturers, quite beyond a reasonable demand for government regard, it suits the purposes of advocacy to call our manufactures infant industries still needing the highest and greatest degree of favor and fostering care, that can be wrung from Federal legislation.[33]

Cleveland, true to the populist tradition, was attacking manufacturers for exploiting the public through manipulating federal legislation. The manufacturers' perversion of public argument also extended to scare tactics—warning of lower wages due to foreign competition:

To these [people who benefit from high tariffs], the appeal is made to save their wages by resisting a change. There should be no disposition to answer such suggestions by the allegation that they are in a minority among those who labor, and therefore should forego an advantage in the interest of low prices for the majority. Their compensation, as it may be affected by the operation of tariff laws, should at all times be scrupulously kept in view; and yet with slight reflection they will not overlook the fact that they are consumers with the rest; that they too have their own wants and those of their families to supply from their earnings, and that the price of the necessaries of life, as well as the amount of their wages, will regulate the measure of their welfare and comfort.[34]

Just as it is difficult to balance the long-term benefits of free trade versus the short-term benefits of protection, it is difficult to balance the immediate prospects of lower wages with the diffuse prospect of lower prices. To emphasize his role as protector of the national interest, Cleveland reassured workers that he would keep their compensation "scrupulously in view." However, this was an issue of laborers against manufacturers—of the people against the machine. That trusts were colluding to keep prices high was evidence that tariffs could, and should, be lower: "The necessity of combination to maintain the price of any commodity to the tariff point furnishes proof that someone is willing to accept lower prices for such commodity and that such prices are remunerative; and lower prices produced by competition prove the same thing. Thus where either of these conditions exist a case would seem to be presented for an easy reduction of taxation."[35]

Manufacturers who colluded through trusts were violating the very principle of the free market—the ideal of capitalism in the form of competition. Cleveland appealed to the members of Congress, as representatives of the national interest, to break free from the grip of trusts: "The difficulty attending a wise and fair revision of our tariff laws is not underestimated. It will require on the part of the Congress great labor and care, and especially a broad and national contemplation of the subject and a patriotic disregard of such local and selfish claims as are unreasonable and reckless of the welfare of the entire country."[36]

While Cleveland disparaged trusts, he was careful to distinguish between, on the one hand, manufacturers colluding to the detriment of the whole and in violation of free market capitalism and, on the other, the economic conditions necessary for manufacturers to make reasonable profits. Whether or not the domestic market was flooded by imports and fair competition prevailed, manufacturers were still overlooking a vital overseas market, where they could take advantage of cheaper imported supplies to make their products and, in turn, sell them abroad for a higher profit. Moreover, foreign outlets assured a more reliable market: "Thus our people might have the opportunity of extending their sales beyond the limits of home consumption, saving them from depression, interruption in business and loss caused by a glutted domestic market and affording their employees more certain and steady labor, with its resulting quiet and contentment."[37] While Cleveland had as his goal trust-busting, he did not have in mind the elimination of all manufacturing. In turn, he implored manufacturers to act for the good of the country and defined the prevailing economic circumstances as constituting a crisis:

Nor can the presentation made of such considerations be with any degree of fairness regarded as evidence of unfriendliness toward our manufacturing interests or of any lack of appreciation of their value and importance.

Those interests constitute a leading and most substantial element of our national greatness and furnish the proud proof of our country's progress. But if in the emergency that presses upon us our manufacturers are asked to surrender something for the public good and to avert disaster, their patriotism as well as a grateful recognition of advantages already afforded should lead them to willing cooperation.[38]

In appealing to Congress, Cleveland made the traditional executive argument that the representatives should disregard their parochial concerns in favor of the national interest: "The question thus imperatively presented for solution should be approached in a spirit higher than partisanship and considered in the light of that regard for patriotic duty which should characterize the action of those entrusted with the weal of a confiding people."[39] Similar to Hamilton's 1831 request, Cleveland defined the excess revenue reaped through tariffs as undue taxation: "The simple and plain duty which we owe the people is to reduce taxation to the necessary expenses of an economical operation of the Government and to restore to the business of the country the money which we hold in the Treasury through the perversion of governmental powers."[40] Consistent with this idea of limited government, Cleveland maintained that all would benefit from the operation of free market capitalism: "These things can and should be done with safety to all our industries, without danger to the opportunity for remunerative labor which our workingmen need, and with benefit to them and all our people by cheapening their means of subsistence and increasing the measure of their comforts."[41]

There was, however, a measured distinction between Cleveland's support for lowering tariffs and contemporary presidential arguments. For Cleveland, the tariff remained the primary source of revenue for the federal government. Thus, he defined the primary issue as one of taxation, deliberately disavowing any controversy over the principle of free trade: "The question of free trade is absolutely irrelevant, and the persistent claim made in certain quarters that all the efforts to relieve the people from unjust and unnecessary taxation are schemes of so-called free traders is mischievous and removed from any consideration for the public good."[42]

In the 1888 presidential campaign, President Cleveland battled William Henry Harrison. Trade was a major issue in the campaign, and Harrison, who favored high tariffs, defeated Cleveland.

The McKinley Bill of 1890: Continued Protection

President Harrison, who was an ardent protectionist, clarified his position on the tariff immediately following his election. On 2 December 1989, the day after Congress opened its session, Harrison spoke in support of expanding tariffs: "The inequalities of the law should be readjusted, but the protective principle should be maintained and fairly applied to the products of our farms as well as of our shops."[43] President Harrison returned to the earlier presidential argument that protection was a device necessary to supporting domestic industries: "These duties necessarily have relation to other things besides the public revenues. We cannot limit their effects by fixing our eyes upon the public Treasury alone. They have a direct relation to home production, to work, to wages, and to the commercial independence of our country, and the wise and patriotic legislator should enlarge the field of his vision to include all of these."[44]

Throughout U.S. history, presidents have typically appealed to legislators to place the national interest above more parochial constituent concerns in support of the principle of free trade. Harrison argued the opposite: he supported giving priority to an extension of the tariff in support of domestic manufacturers securing American jobs, wages, and military security over the principle of free trade. As is typical in trade policy, the vocal minority supporting protection won concessions, aided immeasurably by the support of the president: "Vote-bartering over particular provisions of tariff acts obscured broad principles."[45] More to the point, Harrison expanded the infant industries argument beyond recognition. The bill had the "express purpose of stimulating the introduction of the industry—a policy of fostering the embryo, rather than of protecting the infant; and a proviso was added that the duty should be abrogated altogether in case a specified degree of success should not attend the experiment."[46]

The McKinley Bill of 1890 was also notable for introducing the principle of reciprocity. This bill was a radical change in the tariff system, dramatically increasing duties. Tariffs could be used to pressure foreign nations into allowing U.S. imports; in other words, retaliation in the name of fair trade. Secretary of State James E. Blaine suggested reciprocity in a letter to the president for the purpose of expanding trade with Latin America.[47] President Harrison forwarded the letter to Congress, backing Blaine's proposal for reciprocity and suggesting recommendations for implementation. However, Harrison was unsure whether concessions that had already been made could be retracted: "The real difficulty in the way of negotiating profitable reciprocity treaties is that we have freely given so much that would have had value in the mutual concessions which such treaties imply."[48] Reciprocity has become a cornerstone in the negotiation of trade treaties. It is integral to the expansion of the principle of free trade to include fair trade. The popular notion of the United States as trade patsy is reflected in these early arguments introducing reciprocity.

The Decline of Tariffs and Forced Reciprocity

In the 1890s, the tariff was replaced as the dominant national focus by free silver, war, extracontinental expansion, and trusts. The Democrats were politically weak, and the Republicans regained the White House. The subordination of the tariff issue combined with the force of inertia allowed the high tariff rates set in the 1897 Dingley Bill to last for over a decade. The Dingley Bill endured a four-month debate, with 7/8 of the time in the Senate. It was a Republican restoration of protectionism.

The principle of protection became a right, not an exception. Protection was codified in the 1908 Republican platform, with the introduction of the "true principle": "In all protective legislation the true principle of protection is best maintained by the imposition of such duties as will equal the difference between the cost of production at home and abroad, together with a reasonable profit to American industries."[49] In other words, the true principle ensured that American products would, in all cases, be cheaper than foreign products. It eliminated foreign competition: "It seems to say—no favors, no undue protection; nothing but equalization of conditions. Yet little acumen is needed to see that, carried out consistently, it means simple prohibition and complete stoppage of foreign trade."[50] Despite this economic nullification of the principle of free trade, through emphasis on the term, "reasonable profit," protectionists were able to rhetorically assuage those who favored lower tariffs by implying some diminution in excess profits.

The continued emphasis on the principle of reciprocity was evident in the 1913 Underwood Tariff Act. This act continued the penalty provision of the Payne-Aldrich tariff of 1909. Both allowed the president more flexible powers in adding duties in the case of discrimination by foreign countries. The executive retained control over trade policy, and insofar as he abided by the overarching paradigm—at this time, protectionism via forced reciprocity—the president was allowed the freedom to make minor adjustments in policy: "Executive branch action was still by mutual consent a matter of secondary adjustments to meet changing circumstances."[51] The flexibility allowed by the terms "reasonable profits" and "competitive tariffs" translated into a chameleon trade policy. Republicans, by espousing equal costs, could bar imports. Democrats, by espousing competitive rates, could keep imports coming in: "Whenever there has been a crisis, the free traders or protectionists, as the case may be, have been tempted to use it [the tariff] as a means for overthrowing the system they opposed. As a rule, the tariff system of a country operates neither to cause nor to prevent crises. They are the results of conditions of exchange and production on which it can exercise no great permanent influence."[52] It is monetary policy more than tariff policy that determines the economic health of a nation. The tariff, though, is the easier rhetorical target; it symbolizes the successes or failures of government economic policies.

THE 1930s: REVOLUTION IN TRADE

President Hoover: Trade as Domestic Policy

On 16 June 1930, President Hoover approved the Smoot-Hawley Trade Bill. The Smoot-Hawley Trade Bill, also known as the Tariff Act of 1930, raised U.S. tariffs on over 20,000 items to record levels, contributing to the Great Depression. Hoover embraced the bill as leader of the Republican party, defending it as "a result of pledges given by the Republican Party."[53] Hoover did not merely support Smoot-Hawley as a matter of partisan obligation, he adamantly endorsed the legislation for its ability to minimize the influence of special interest groups through the flexible tariff provision. He also let stand the legislative responsibility for setting tariffs on specific items: "Certainly no President, with his other duties, can pretend to make that exhaustive determination of the complex facts which surround each of those 3,300 items, and which has required the attention of hundreds of men in Congress for nearly a year and a third. That responsibility must rest upon the Congress in a legislative rate revision."[54]

Having ostensibly let the ultimate responsibility for establishing tariffs remain with Congress, Hoover in effect bypassed this body. He explained that the flexible tariff would automatically adjust tariffs in the best interests of the nation, sparing the legislature this tedious, and hereafter unnecessary, task:

On the administrative side I have insisted, however, that there should be created a new basis for the flexible tariff and it has been incorporated in this law. Thereby the means are established for objective and judicial review of these rates upon principles laid down by the Congress, free from pressures inherent in legislative action. Thus, the outstanding step of this tariff legislation has been the reorganization of the largely inoperative flexible provision of 1922 into a form which should render it possible to secure prompt and scientific adjustment of serious inequities and inequalities which may prove to have been incorporated in the bill.[55]

Hoover argued that the flexible tariff would eliminate the pressure of special interests lobbying the legislative branch while, more importantly, allowing for the adjustment of tariffs to meet changing circumstances.

This new provision has even a larger importance. If a perfect tariff bill were enacted today, the increased rapidity of economic change and the constant shifting of our relations to industries abroad [would] create a continuous stream of items which would work hardship upon some segment of the American people except for the provision of this relief. Without a workable flexible provision we would require even more frequent congressional tariff revision than during the past. With it the country should be freed from further general revision for many years to come. Congressional revisions are not only disturbing to business but with all their necessary collateral surroundings in lobbies, log rolling, and the activities of group interests, are disturbing to the public confidence.[56]

However, while asserting that congressional control would remain over setting tariffs via a reorganized Tariff Commission composed of bipartisan legislators, Hoover retained final veto power over the commission's conclusions. In effect, this nullified legislative control: "Recommendations are to be made to the President, he being given authority to promulgate or veto the conclusions of the Commission."[57] Hoover argued that passage of the flexible tariff was critical in order to allow appropriate levels of tariffs while removing the process from the corruption of special interests:

As I have said, I do not assume the rate structure in this or any other tariff bill is perfect, but I am convinced that the disposal of the whole question is urgent. I believe that the flexible provisions can within reasonable time remedy inequalities; that this provision is a progressive advance and gives great hope of taking the tariff away from politics, lobbying, and log rolling; that the bill gives protection to agriculture for the market of its products and to several industries in need of such protection for the wage of their labor; that with returning normal conditions our foreign trade will continue to expand.[58]

In his enthusiastic embrace of the flexible tariff provision, Hoover failed to recognize the blatant political influences on tariffs established by the Smoot-Hawley Bill. With the Democrats regaining control of the House in 1930, Hoover faced even greater congressional opposition to his trade policy. On 11 May 1932, he vetoed a bill lowering tariffs by 35 percent. Announcing the veto, Hoover argued that House Resolution (HR) 6662 was not needed and was actually dangerous, as it destroyed the flexible tariff:

My first objection to the bill is the misimpression and uncertainty it may convey as to its purpose. If the purpose of the proponents of this act is to secure lower tariffs on the 35 percent of our imports which are not on the free list it would seem that the direct and simple method of so doing would be to recognize that tariffs are duties applied to particular commodities, and to propose definite reduction of the duties on such particular commodities as are believed to be at fault and upon which the full facts can be developed. Alternatively, the Congress is able to direct the Tariff Commission under the "flexible" provisions of the act of 1930 to act upon such schedules as are believed to be too high. As a matter of fact there never has been a time in the history of the United States when tariff protection was more essential to the welfare of the American people than at present.[59]

President Hoover placed inordinate emphasis on the importance of tariff legislation to the U.S. welfare and he fervently argued that the high tariffs established by the Tariff Act of 1930 were essential to America's economic recovery. He further argued that lowering tariffs artificially—in effect, nullifying the flexible tariff provision—would renew special interests' influence on the legislative process and, ultimately, would eliminate domestic control over trade:

This bill would destroy the effectiveness of the flexible tariff which for the first time gives protection against excessive or inadequate tariffs, prevents a system of frozen tariffs upon the country irrespective of economic change and gives relief from log rolling and politics in tariff making. It would surrender our own control of an important part of our domestic affairs to the influence of other nations or alternatively would lead us into futilities in international negotiations. It would start our country upon the road of a system of preferential tariffs between nations with all the trade wars, international entanglements, etc., which our country has sought to avoid by extending equal treatment to all of them.[60]

The arguments Hoover made are consistent with the rhetorical tradition of the executive branch on trade policy. He argued for congressional agreement with his position in the name of assuring presidential strength in international negotiations and to alleviate unwarranted—and potentially harmful—special interest pressure on the legislative branch. However, Hoover was the last president to make these arguments in favor of high tariffs. Future executives would instead point to the Smoot-Hawley Bill (which Hoover had defined as the savior of trade politics), as evidence of the devastating effects of high tariffs. Smoot-Hawley is now a rhetorical symbol of the negative consequences of protectionism and, in this instance, its effect in propelling the United States into the Great Depression. The Smoot-Hawley Bill marks a transition in trade rhetoric. Hoover was the last president to define trade as solely a domestic issue and the last to favor high tariffs.

President Franklin Roosevelt: Trade as Foreign Policy

With the election of Roosevelt, the focus of trade policy changed from import politics—restricting imports through tariff legislation—to export politics—focusing on opening up foreign markets. Trade was thus more intimately connected with the president's treaty-making powers. This change from an import- to an export-based trade policy was understandable given America's increasing economic power. In its early years as a republic, the country needed to establish its domestic manufacturing base as well as its political independence. However, as manufacturing became self-sufficient and then entered into excess production, foreign markets became more desirable. Moreover, as domestic standards of living improved, imports were needed in greater number. There was a mutual interest in increased trade and in free trade without barriers.[61] As a result, the principle of reciprocity came to the forefront in trade negotiations. Presidential trade rhetoric now had to balance pressing for open markets—ensuring free trade—with congressional interests—demanding fair trade.

The Trade and Tariff Act of 1934. By 1934 the tariff served immensely different purposes than the original Tariff of 1789. In 1913 the Sixteenth Amendment established the income tax, which became the major source of government revenue. By 1920 the tariff was used exclusively for protectionist purposes. When Great Britain departed from the gold standard in 1931, the tariff further declined in importance as an instrument in U.S. trade regulation.

Franklin Roosevelt vigorously pushed for a liberal free trade policy, using as rhetorical justification its role in promoting peace. His secretary of state, Cordell Hull, who was a proponent of free trade and had introduced free trade legislation as a congressman in 1916, coordinated the administration's push for liberalized trade. During the Roosevelt administration, the Export-Import Bank (Eximbank) was established under the authority of the National Industrial Recovery Act of 1933. Its purpose was to finance U.S. exports so as to maintain their competitiveness. Eximbank's strategy was to shift expenditures in foreign countries toward goods produced in the United States, thus maintaining and enlarging foreign markets for U.S. agriculture, industry, mining, and manufacturing products. On the domestic front, the 1933 Buy American Act mandated that domestic goods be bought for defense purposes if available at reasonable costs.

However, the most important piece of trade legislation was the 1934 Reciprocal Trade Agreements Act, which authorized the president to negotiate mutual reductions in tariff rates, thus allowing a mild broadening of presidential powers. This assumption of executive power, which had at first been an exception, now became the rule. Congress did not fill the void by voting adjustments in tariff levels, and indeed, specific tariff rates that were proposed in the legislature were voted down. In effect, Congress resisted the responsibilities involved in managing tariffs, as predicted by Hoover in advocating his ill-fated flexible tariff. In abdicating power to the executive branch, the legislature was able to minimize its constituencies' clamor for protectionism: "Responsibility brings with it intolerable pressure. The power to dole out favors to industry is not worth the price of having to beat off and placate the insistent pleas of petitioners."[62]

The Reciprocal Trade Agreements Act established a bargaining tariff, an executive broker, quasi-judicial trade remedies, special deals, and strong congressional committees with liberal executive leaders. With the responsibility for trade policy delegated to the executive branch, the "cry-and-sigh syndrome"—also known as the "bicycle theory"—became the rhetorical model for trade negotiations.[63]

The Cry-and-Sigh Syndrome. The cry-and-sigh syndrome is a name for the symbolic interaction between Congress and the president in trade politics. Congress argues for protection, and the president uses this congressional pressure to persuade foreign nations to open markets. Congress is able to propose legislative action, the President uses these bills as signs of congressional and, thus, public discontent; as a result, open markets are achieved without protectionist legislation.

During negotiations with foreign countries, the argument for protection is at its weakest, as imposing import restrictions tends to undercut talks aimed at broadening American trade advantages. However, congressional pressure resulting from constituent petitions may work at odds with national interests. As a result, Congress has delegated power to the executive to facilitate treaty making while allowing the legislative body to clamor for protection without suffering the consequences of actual punitive, trade-restricting measures: "Individual members also remained free to make ample protectionist noise, to declaim loudly on behalf of producer interests that were strong in their states or districts. In fact, they could do so more freely than ever, secure in the knowledge that most actual decisions would be made elsewhere."[64]

This rhetorical game has continued ever since Congress established these broad parameters for presidential actions in the 1930s. The president can change tariff levels, modify procedures, and define exceptions. While Congress retains the right to vote for statutory trade restrictions, the Smoot-Hawley Trade Act of 1930 was the last general tariff law passed by Congress.

Because of this mutual influence, the success of U.S. trade policy is dependent on the degree of responsiveness and trust between the two branches of government, each of which dominates different levels of the trade policy process. The executive branch prefers having as few laws on trade as possible and has kept industry-specific protection out of the trade statutes. It tends to grant rhetorical leeway to the legislative branch and to "let congressmen play the role they [prefer:] that of making noise, lobbying

the executive branch for action but refraining from final action themselves."[65] The key element in the cry-and-sigh syndrome is this rhetorical
game. Congressional sponsorship of protectionist legislation is not equivalent to support for protectionist actions.

A congressman, no matter how keen his desire to help the toy marble-makers, does
not want to be given the right of voting them an increase in tariff rates. He prefers
to be in the position of being allowed merely to place a speech in their favor in *The
Congressional Record* as an extension of his remarks or to appear as a witness
before the Tariff Commission, free to indulge the irresponsibility afforded those
who do not participate in the final decision. Rather than rule on the plea himself,
he prefers to debate and vote on legislation that sets general principles governing
how the marble-makers' plea should be considered. If he is a protectionist, he wants
those principles lax; if a free trader, rigid—but both agree that Congressional
decision on particulars should be avoided.[66]

The president has an advantage when legislation is limited. There is a
"fundamental Executive preference for as few laws as possible, because as
soon as the policy moves to the congressional arena, the chances are that
the Executive prerogative will be circumscribed."[67] The executive preference for few laws combines with congressional preference to be held
unaccountable for specific tariff decisions to limit broad legislative changes
in tariff policy.

POST–WORLD WAR II

American economic strength was at its apogee following World War II.
The managed-trade practices of Nazi Germany, the embargoes and quotas
on vital materials in World War II, currency and import controls, and the
coordination of U.S. trade policy with foreign political policy all contributed to a decline in the importance of the tariff. The tariff remains potent,
however, if not as an instrument of trade policy then as a rhetorical symbol
brandished by both free traders and protectionists: "It might well be argued
that today the tariff is no longer a major element in the conduct of United
States' foreign trade. Nonetheless, it clearly remains the symbol of protection to both its friends and enemies."[68]

Both the executive and legislative branches supported free trade from
1945 until the late 1960s. The 1944 Bretton Woods agreement set the rules
and the structure for post–World War II international trade policy by
establishing the General Agreement on Tariffs and Trade (GATT) and the
International Monetary Fund (IMF). It was a time for building alliances,

and the relative prosperity of the United States encouraged its leadership role in the formation of international institutions such as GATT and the United Nations. These new alliances were not viewed as unwarranted political entanglements because the United States controlled them: "America's increasing integration into the world was masked by its overwhelming dominance of it."[69] Little changed in trade policy during these years, and the Reciprocal Trade Agreements Act was renewed eight times between 1937 and 1953.

SUMMARY OF ECONOMIC ARGUMENTS

Consistency was the hallmark for arguments, both for and against free trade, in U.S. trade policy. The foundation of free trade rhetoric was the economic theory of the free market, in which trade was profitable when based on comparative advantage. The theory of comparative advantage, as refined by David Ricardo in 1817, held that free trade was mutually profitable given the conditions of specialization, equilibrium in exchange rates, and a competitive market. Only one of these conditions, however, has remained consistently present in worldwide markets—that of specialization. This refers to the ability of nations to manufacture products at an economic advantage because of local circumstances. The second two components—equilibrium in exchange rates and a competitive market—have not always been present.

Free trade advocates have qualified their arguments throughout U.S. history. Even John Stuart Mill admitted the necessity of protecting new industries from imports.[70] The infant industries argument became the foundation for economic nationalism in the late nineteenth century as industries that had been given temporary protection pushed to maintain tariffs. Laissez-faire markets can lead to social dislocations and a lack of job security in the following circumstances: in establishing new industries, in times of transition, in times of unfair trade, and, increasingly, in an interdependent world. As markets become more interdependent, government intervention becomes more necessary to smooth market transitions.

A minimalist role for government might be appropriate in an economy that was sheltered from international competition. It might also be appropriate in an economy that was growing so quickly that structural adjustments were relatively easy—so that, for example, new job and investment opportunities were readily available to replace old ones. But such is not the case. A laissez-faire approach is both naive and dangerous for a national economy with slow growth and for a nation within an interdependent world economy that is prone to sharp and often sudden changes in supply, demand, technology, and politics. Active government policies are necessary to enable the economy to respond quickly and efficiently to world-wide structural changes.[71]

It is, therefore, not surprising that the United States never practiced a pure form of free trade but rather followed a policy of relative openness with "significant and expandable" exceptions.[72] Nevertheless, presidents have remained true to the ideal of free trade while allowing exceptions in the name of fair trade. In their trade rhetoric, they have argued that select protectionist actions were deviations from an overarching policy of free trade and, moreover, were only temporary, to be removed once foreign obstacles to free trade had been dismantled.

Protection has also been allowed as necessary in the name of the national defense and has been maintained for industries manufacturing needed supplies and domestic goods, to ensure a home market for agriculture, and to allow for lower prices in protected industries. However, war is not the ordinary state of domestic politics. The infant industries argument was thus the axiom most readily available to warp to protectionism's advantage. As basic industries became established, the character of the debate changed: "The tone of that protectionist argument was optimistic, aggressive, expansionist. It contrasts with the conservative, static, defensive themes in protectionist arguments today."[73]

The conservative and defensive nature of protectionist arguments permeated the rhetoric of free traders as they adopted the language of reciprocity. In the name of fair trade, if U.S. markets were to be open to imports, other nations had to open their markets to U.S. exports. The principle of reciprocity is extremely powerful because it resonates with an inherent nationalism. Moreover, it seems only fair that concessions should be met by like concessions:

No matter how much weight is given to influence that may have led governments at times to accept less compensation in tariff negotiations than would be suggested by a dollar-for-dollar interpretation of reciprocity, their consistent obeisance to the concept confirms that it is at least a political reality with which they must reckon. They cannot ignore the pervasive belief that, when a country grants a tariff concession, it incurs a cost that must be compensated.[74]

It is not surprising that reciprocity has been the dominant theme in American trade rhetoric: "Opposition to discrimination in international trade has been the central theme of American commercial policy almost from the beginning of the nation. Washington proclaimed it in his Farewell

Address. John Quincy Adams publicly explained that American deviations from this basic principle were 'essentially defensive and counteracting to similar regulations operating against us.' "75

In the latter half of the nineteenth century, the United States began its program of granting most favored nation status. Eventually, most favored nation status would be primarily noted for tying economic concessions to political conditions, yet at the outset, its main purpose was to exact reciprocal treatment of exports. By the 1930s, the United States had moved from a policy of nondiscriminatory trade to one of bilateral agreements. In the 1930s and the 1940s, Britain was a major target for the elimination of discriminatory treatment.

This evolution in trade policy cannot be explained by economic theory alone. Political considerations often take precedence over economic justifications:

No single explanation will cover all the circumstances that cause governments to resist reductions in their tariffs. Efforts to favor special domestic interests, concern with the distribution of real income, temporary balance of payments considerations, even the vestigal influence of long-dead schools of economic thought—all play their part. But all of these domestic concerns together will not explain the persistence of tariff bargaining on the part of countries that could profit from unilateral tariff reductions.[76]

While immediate gains may not be apparent in tariff reductions, long-term strategic goals may be the primary motivation:

It is here suggested that the existence of tariff bargaining is in itself a sufficient reason for the insistence on reciprocity; anticipation of a future need for negotiating power provides incentive enough for hard present bargaining. Thus, the cost a government incurs when it reduces or binds a tariff may be measured less by any possible disadvantages from increased imports than by the value it believes a negotiating partner would place on that action. Once this simple, and observable, fact is recognized, it becomes less difficult to understand how a number of governments intent on the reduction of tariffs for their mutual benefit can be diverted from that purpose into a contest in which each seems as much concerned with denying benefits to its partners as with obtaining benefits for itself.[77]

It is the immediate impact that is most discernible to the public, whether it amounts to increases or decreases in tariff levels. This disconnection between the economic and political rationales for trade policy goes far in explaining the arguments in trade rhetoric. The traditional presidential argument for free but fair trade inherently allows for exceptions in policy. There have been five economic arguments that have warranted the consideration of tariffs (albeit in limited cases and on a temporary basis): providing for revenue, establishing infant industries, negotiating terms of trade, second-best use, and balance of payments.[78] However, most of these once-worthy exceptions are no longer valid. For example, a tariff levied for the purpose of raising revenue is no longer relevant for highly developed countries. In the United States, it became irrelevant in 1913 with the passage of the Sixteenth Amendment, which established the federal income tax. The infant industries argument is also extinct in the highly developed U.S. economy. The terms of trade argument is an economic mistake because one-sided tariffs tend to be imposed, which invites retaliation. The second-best use of tariffs, which promises to match other countries' tariffs, effectively eliminates free trade. Finally, using tariffs to adjust balance-of-payments deficits negatively affects the monetary scale, especially with prolonged use.

Even though these exceptions for tariffs are no longer valid, all once had some merit. However, this is not the case with the flexible tariff or tariffs used to protect wages. The flexible tariff was the principle behind the U.S. Tariff Acts of 1922 and 1930, the intent of which was to offset differences in cost between foreign and domestic producers. In effect, this would eliminate all trade by ignoring the principle of comparative advantage. The second instance—using tariffs to protect domestic wages—also ignores basic economic principles of free trade. Not only does it ignore the causal relationship between productivity and wages, it prevents efficient flow of capital as it hinders exchanges between nations.

While the founding fathers adhered to the ideal of free trade, they did not hesitate to practice a policy of protection in the name of establishing infant industries. The United States was not unique in this regard: "In the real world, almost everybody sees benefits in economic nationalism. Excepting the pioneer, England, every country has developed behind protective barriers."[79] Despite a consistent executive rhetoric espousing the virtues of free trade, a policy of free trade has been practiced historically only when in a country's interest. The United States followed a protectionist policy in its early stages, as a developing country, and in its mid-stages, as an exclusionist economy. It was not until a period of postwar fervor, during which the nation became an economic power, that free trade came into ascendancy.

NOTES

1. See Edward Stanwood, *American Tariff Controversies in the Nineteenth Century*, 1st ed., 2 vols. (New York: Russell and Russell, 1903).

2. Alexander Hamilton, John Jay, and James Madison, *The Federalist* (New York: Heritage Press, 1945), 18.

3. Stanwood, *American Tariff Controversies*, 1st ed., 11.

4. Ibid., 28.

5. F. W. Taussig, *The Tariff History of the United States*, 7th ed. (New York: G. P. Putnam's Sons, 1923), 14.

6. Stanwood, *American Tariff Controversies*, 1st ed., 76.

7. F. W. Taussig, *State Papers and Speeches on the Tariff* (Clifton, N.J.: Augustus M. Kelley Publishers, 1972), 30.

8. Ibid., 31.

9. Stanwood, *American Tariff Controversies*, 1st ed., 126.

10. Raymond Bauer, Ithiel de Sola Pool, and Lewis Anthony Dexter, *American Business and Public Policy* (Chicago: Aldine-Atherton, 1972), 19.

11. Taussig, *Tariff History*, 16.

12. F. W. Taussig, *Some Aspects of the Tariff Question*, vol. 7 of *Harvard Economic Studies* (Cambridge: Harvard University Press, 1915), 20.

13. Ibid., 21.

14. Ibid., 24.

15. Ibid., 25–26.

16. Bauer, Pool, and Dexter, *American Business*, 12.

17. Stanwood, *American Tariff Controversies*, 1st ed., 200–201.

18. Ibid., 201.

19. Ibid., 202–203.

20. Ibid., 360–361.

21. Ibid.

22. Ibid.

23. Ibid., 369–370.

24. Ibid.

25. Ibid.

26. Ibid., 389–390.

27. Ibid.

28. Ibid., 391.

29. Ibid., 402.

30. *House Miscellaneous Document no. 210*, 53rd Cong., 2nd sess., in *Compilation of the Messages and Papers of the Presidents, 1789–1987*, ed. J. D. Richardson (Washington, D.C.: U.S. Government Printing Office, 1910), 11:5169.

31. Ibid., 5170.

32. Ibid., 5169.

33. Ibid., 5170.

34. Ibid., 5171.

35. Ibid., 5173.

36. Ibid., 5174.

37. Ibid.

38. Ibid., 5173–5174.

39. Ibid., 5174–5175.

40. Ibid., 5175.

41. Ibid.

42. Ibid.

43. Stanwood, *American Tariff Controversies*, 2nd ed., 259.

44. Ibid.

45. Bauer, Pool, and Dexter, *American Business*, 16–17.

46. Stanwood, *American Tariff Controversies*, 2nd ed., 264.

47. See ibid., 276.

48. Ibid., 277.

49. Taussig, *Tariff History*, 363.

50. Ibid.

51. Bauer, Pool, and Dexter, *American Business*, 36–37.

52. Taussig, *Tariff History*, 120.

53. Herbert Hoover, *Public Papers of the Presidents of the United States* (Washington, D.C.: Office of the Federal Register, National Archives and Records Service, 1931), 231.

54. Hoover, *Public Papers 1930*, 232–233.

55. Ibid.

56. Ibid., 233.

57. Ibid., 232–234.

58. Ibid., 235.

59. Hoover, *Public Papers 1932–1933*, 205.

60. Ibid., 210.

61. See Stanley D. Metzger, *Trade Agreements and the Kennedy Round* (Fairfax, Va.: Corner Publications, 1964), 11–12.

62. Bauer, Pool, and Dexter, *American Business*, 37.

63. Allen Schick, *Making Economic Policy in Congress* (Washington, D.C.: American Enterprise Institute, 1983), 160–161.

64. I. M. Destler, *American Trade Politics* (Washington, D.C.: Institute for International Economics and the Twentieth Century Fund, 1986), 13.

65. Ibid., 25.

66. Ibid., 38.

67. Robert A. Pastor, *Congress and the Politics of U.S. Foreign Economic Policy 1929–1976* (Berkeley: University of California Press, 1980), 54.

68. Bauer, Pool, and Dexter, *American Business*, 18–19.

69. Robert B. Reich, *Tales of a New America* (New York: Random House, 1987), 53.

70. Richard Thomas Cupitt, *Domestic Political and Economic Instability and International Trade Policy* (Athens: University of Georgia Press, 1985), 19.

71. Ira C. Magaziner and Robert B. Reich, *Minding America's Business* (New York: Vantage Books, 1983), 331.

72. Destler, *American Trade Politics,* 31–32.

73. Bauer, Pool, and Dexter, *American Business*, 14.

74. John W. Evans, *The Kennedy Round in American Trade Policy* (Cambridge: Harvard University Press, 1971), 24–25.

75. Ibid., 32–33.

76. Ibid.

77. Ibid.

78. Ibid., 23–30.

79. B. Bruce Briggs, "The Coming Overthrow of Free Trade," *Wall Street Journal*, 24 February 1983, 28.

Chapter Two

Trade in the Era of the Cold War: Maintaining and Building Political Alliances

Following World War II, the United States pursued free trade, even if economically disadvantageous, to promote international development: "The United States was prepared to postpone direct trade advantages in favor of speeding the recovery of a world disrupted by war and, more particularly, the economic recovery of Europe, both for reasons of security and to reduce the cost of the Marshall Plan."[1] The argument was between politicians and statesmen.[2] Foreign policy statesmen were more likely to accept the negative domestic economic consequences of using free trade as a diplomatic tool. There was "an inherent value struggle in international economic policy: domestic economics versus foreign political considerations."[3]

Thus, at the height of the Cold War era and during a time of American economic dominance, trade policy was used as a tool for establishing, building, and maintaining political alliances. The United States could afford to bestow generous trading privileges. U.S. presidents followed a policy of privately pursuing free trade pacts, with Congress continuing to grant the executive branch prerogative in formulating trade policy. Nonetheless, the direction of trade policy during this period was not stagnant. U.S. economic strength declined, and although the economy remained strong, trade policy was no longer accepted as an expendable element in the geopolitical game.

In the 1960s and 1970s, Presidents John Kennedy and Richard Nixon both pursued trade pacts; Kennedy successfully and Nixon unsuccessfully. The two trade pacts reflected this change in economic strength and policy. While both presidents asked for increased negotiating authority, the two men were reacting to distinct political and economic circumstances. Kennedy was faced with the decline in U.S. gold reserves and the increasing economic power of the European Economic Community. Nixon was faced with a decline in the U.S. trade surplus and, as a result, congressional pressure for restrictions on trade. He advocated augmenting trade-adjustment assistance programs, arguing that the program—begun with the 1960 trade pact—was not strong enough.

One of the most marked changes in international trade policy was the evolution from bilateral trade agreements to regional trading blocs, as manifested by the European Common Market. Domestically and internationally, increasing restrictions were placed on trade. In the United States, presidents justified such measures in the name of fair trade. Throughout all the economic and political changes, however, they remained committed to the principle of free trade.

THE TRADE EXPANSION ACT OF 1962

Economic and Political Context

By June 1962, the Trade Act (an extension of the Reciprocal Trade Agreements Act, which had been renewed regularly since 1934) was due to expire and the Kennedy administration wanted a new bill with an expansion of presidential powers. The administration's intent was to further institutionalize free trade policies.

The formation of the European Common Market was a motivating force behind Kennedy's push for the 1962 Trade Expansion Act. The treaty establishing the European Economic Community (EEC)—the Treaty of Rome—was signed on 25 March 1957. The Common Market included France, West Germany, Italy, Belgium, the Netherlands, and Luxembourg. Moreover, in 1962 there was the very real possibility that Great Britain would join (Britain's membership was ultimately rejected by Charles De-Gaulle in 1963 who was EEC president of finance). The Kennedy administration supported the Common Market for two reasons. First, this economic alliance had the potential to eliminate the animosity between France and Germany, and second, a more economically efficient, combined market had the potential to become a larger market for American exports.

However, there was also the threat that a united market would exclude American products. Nonetheless, the Kennedy administration, viewed the opportunity for promoting exports to the EEC as greater than the risk of the potential imposition of import barriers by the European member nations.

When the 1962 trade agreements legislation was planned, the dominating motive remained what it had been in 1958: to reduce the discrimination against American exports, both industrial and agricultural, which would increase as the Common Market's customs union reached its completion. If anything, this motive had been intensified by the real concern which had been aroused by the Common Market's newly-announced agricultural policy, which threatened to curtail drastically American exports of over $1 billion annually of agricultural products to Europe.[4]

The potential addition of Great Britain, however, seemed to promise a more liberalized EEC trading policy. Moreover, even with trading preferences granted between partners, the expansion of the market would offset such preferences:

Clearly, an expansion of the European Community carried some economic risks for the United States. An enlarged Community meant a greater area of preferential treatment, to the disadvantage of U.S. exports, at least in the short run. But there were potential economic advantages as well. When the United Kingdom took its seat in the council of the Community, there was a good chance that it would cast its weight on the side of a liberal trading policy. It was generally accepted that Germany and the Netherlands favored maximum trade with the outside world. They also had shown themselves most anxious to welcome the United Kingdom as a partner. The three together, it was thought, would wield decisive power in Community deliberations. And if a genuinely liberal approach to external trade were adopted, the resulting reductions in the level of protection against outsiders might more than offset the additional trade preferences to be created between Britain and its EEC partners.[5]

While the potential inclusion of Britain in the EEC was a credible economic rationale for promoting the Trade Expansion Act of 1962, it was more valuable for its rhetorical potential in justifying an expansion of presidential powers:

Although abortive, the British application for membership served one purpose that did produce lasting results. It provided an ideal background for the President's request for new powers in the trade field. Without this new element, it would have been difficult for President Kennedy to inject into his request the necessary sense of urgency, at least while the outcome of the Dillon Round [the fifth round of trade negotiations under GATT] was uncertain. With the prospect of a greatly enlarged Community, however, the administration could present a compelling argument for asking for power to take new and more heroic measures before it was too late.[6]

The success of the EEC, as reflected in its accumulation of gold and foreign exchange, was also problematic because it coincided with the increasing trade imbalance in the United States. It was the depletion of the gold reserves at Fort Knox, with a loss of $4.7 billion from 1958 to 1960, that best symbolized the U.S. economic decline: the depletion had previously been ignored because it was, in effect, buried in the arcane economic language of U.S. balance of payments statistics. In a seeming reversal of fortunes, during the same three years—following the formation of the EEC in 1958—the six nations comprising the community had increased their monetary reserves by over $6.5 billion. In addition, the EEC nations' combined gross national product (GNP) exceeded the U.S. GNP by more than two to one, yet another indication of the former group's attraction for foreign investors.[7]

President Kennedy almost immediately took action to reduce the balance-of-payments deficit. In a special message to Congress given three weeks after taking office, on 6 February 1961, Kennedy was careful to avoid defining the situation as a crisis: "Our situation is one that justifies concern but not panic or alarm."[8] In this new Democratic, activist government, Kennedy was taking measured steps to manage the economy. In his words: "In sum our basic deficit of $1.5 billion is of manageable proportions. And it is the basic deficit which affects the real strength of our currency. But the time has come to end this deficit. It must be ended by responsible, determined and constructive measures." First, the administration backed the dollar with gold at $35 an ounce. Second, the outflow of U.S. dollars would be monitored and limited to reaffirm control over the balance-of-payments position. Third, the administration would continue former President Dwight Eisenhower's efforts to encourage exports. Kennedy asserted that his administration would place "maximum emphasis on expanding our exports. Our costs and prices must therefore be kept low; and the government must play a more vigorous part in helping to enlarge foreign markets for American goods and services." Fourth, protectionist measures were considered counterproductive. To realign the balance-of-payments position, the United States would promote exports, rather than restrict imports. Kennedy remained in the executive position of supporting free trade and stated: "A return to protectionism is not the solution. Such a course would provoke retaliation; and the balance of trade, which is now substantially in our favor, could be turned against us with disastrous effects to the dollar." Fifth, Kennedy pledged to increase aid to the developing countries, out of both economic and political necessity. The dictum, "trade, not aid" remained relevant to the formation of U.S. trade policy, as did the interrelation of economic and foreign policy. Kennedy stated:

The flow of resources from the industrialized countries to the developing countries must be increased. In all that we do to strengthen our balance of payments, we must be especially mindful that the less developed countries remain in a weak financial position. Help from the industrialized countries is more important than ever; we cannot strengthen our balance of payments at the expense of the developing countries without incurring even greater dangers to our national security.

In this Cold War mindset, the battle between the Soviet Union and the United States over control of the developing countries was ever present. Finally, Kennedy stressed the importance of U.S. economic leadership—of a benevolence mandated by the U.S. position in international affairs: "The United States must take the lead in harmonizing the financial and economic policies for growth and stability of those industrialized nations of the world whose economic behavior significantly influences the course of the world economy and the trend of international payments."

President Kennedy's desire to expand trade coalesced with his attempt to expand presidential powers, all of which was in line with executive tradition. Kennedy wanted to expand trade through exports in order to decrease the balance-of-payments deficit. Thus, the administration began a persuasive campaign—both public and private—for passage of the Trade Expansion Act of 1962.

The Public Campaign

The nature of trade policy—most notably, the desire to avoid activating the latent protectionist public, which had been aggravated by the growing strength of the European Common Market—when combined with the relatively late decision by the Kennedy administration to push for a major new trade bill, seemed to militate against successful passage of the act. Nonetheless, the administration mounted an "intensively and skillfully managed" and, most important, effectively persuasive campaign.[9]

When the administration did go public, it did so in a limited way: "The Kennedy strategy went as far in the direction of avoiding broad public agitation as was possible. The strategy was to negotiate with particular industrial groups to meet their objections and pull the sting of their opposition in advance."[10] With the initial proposals, the Kennedy administration relied on the support of such notable figures, as William Clayton, who was undersecretary of state under Harry Truman and Christian Herter, Eisenhower's secretary of state. It was not until May that the administration again went public. In the intervening months, it relied instead on congressional hearings for low-key publicity.

In May, a month before hoped-for House action, there was again a burst of presidential speeches, Washington conferences, and World Trade Week activities. Public House hearings through late winter and early spring served their function, however, of forcing the discussion of the issue into the press and the public arena. A strategy of quiet elite persuasion could be maintained only up to a point. In summary, we see that, in the instance of trade legislation, as in many instances in the study of public opinion, it is more important to look at which part of the public is activated than at which is converted.[11]

Public opinion on trade policy tends to be unstable. Because trade is generally not an important issue to the public, there exists highly general underlying attitudes. While there is ongoing public support for the notion of fairness (as translated into the principle of reciprocity), preservation of the status quo remains the mainstay of trade policy. Historically, trade has been one of the major issues separating Republicans and Democrats. This does not mean that the parties have historically supported the same position. Rather, they have shifted stances as their membership has evolved in educational level and income, with better-educated citizens prone to favor free trade. In theory, free trade benefits all citizens as consumers, as it results in superior products at competitive prices, regardless of the existence of fair trade. Perhaps more important, educated citizens pay increased attention to political issues, and conventional wisdom, irrespective of constituent pressure, favors free trade, even while rhetorically demanding fair trade.

Individual income level has been a weaker predictor of stance on trade than educational level.[12] Industry affiliation cuts across lines of education, party, and political activity: "Speaking of the population as a whole, we can say that the strongest support for protectionism comes from those people who are older than average, have less than a high school education, are factory workers, vote Democratic, and are relatively low in political activity. The strongest opponents of protectionism are young, college trained, wealthy, Republican, and politically active."[13]

Arousing among the public those who are politically inactive activates the very segment supporting protectionism. Therefore, a discussion of trade will result in an apparent popular swing in that direction. Congress is especially sensitive to constituency pressure, often via the arousal of special interest groups: "A relatively few voices, well exercised, sometimes created the impression of unified community sentiment. Public spokesmen, be they congressmen or others, have a sharp ear, attuned to complaints that foreshadow discontent. They react, not to actual opinion, but to their image of what opinion could become if not forestalled by action on their part."[14]

Thus, vocal minorities may offset the more politically involved citizens' support for free trade: "On the whole, those Americans who are interested, aware, and have an opinion on the subject, have switched from a protectionist doctrine to what appears to be a predominant support for a liberal position. As in the past, the potential support resting in the citizen body may be entirely offset by the political activity of relatively small groups with particular and immediate stakes in the issue."[15]

Designed to avoid activating the protectionist public while at the same time beginning to alert Congress of impending action, the initial strategy of the Kennedy administration involved launching three trial balloons.[16] First, Representative Hale Boggs (D–La.), upon returning from a European excursion, declared that a simple extension of the trade agreements legislation—due to expire in June 1962—would not be adequate, because, in his words, it was "grossly ineffective in dealing with the common economic front of Western Europe."[17]

Second, in a speech before the National Foreign Trade Council, George Ball, who would become Undersecretary of State for Economic Affairs for Kennedy, stated that the new circumstances of the EEC required an innovative U.S. response and asked for negotiating authority "sufficiently broad in scope to meet the opportunity and challenge of the European Economic Community."[18] Ball defined the necessary change as moving beyond item-by-item negotiations.

Third, the administration relied on the testimony of two notable former government officials, Christian A. Herter and Will Clayton. The statesmen called for cooperation with the EEC: "We believe that the United States must form a partnership with the European Common Market and take the leadership in expanding a free world economic community."[19]

President Kennedy's major public initiative occurred on 8 November via the rhetorical forum of a news conference. Kennedy stressed that the EEC presented both opportunities and risks, but that potential danger also lay in U.S. inaction: "My judgment is that the time to begin is now. One-third of our trade generally is in Western Europe, and if the United States should be denied that market we will either find a flight of capital from this country to construct factories within that wall, or we will find ourselves in serious economic trouble."[20]

Public hearings on the Trade Expansion Act began in the House on 4 December 1961. In the legislative halls the administration worked in concert with congressional leaders.

Traditionally, in tariff matters the legislative machinery begins to turn with hearings before the Ways and Means Committee of the House of Representatives. Formal congressional examination of the bill that was to become the Trade Expansion Act followed the normal pattern. But more than a month before the administration's proposals had been submitted to the Congress, Representative Boggs and the influential subcommittee he headed were already playing a role in the campaign of education and persuasion. The subcommittee opened its public hearings on December 4, 1961, with statements by Governor Herter and Mr. Clayton.[21]

There was no grand public campaign for the Trade Expansion Act of 1962, but rather a limited strategy coordinating legislative hearings, expert testimony, and presidential support. Kennedy's major persuasive initiative centered on co-opting the opposition (mainly business and labor).

The Private Campaign

Coincident with these House hearings, on 6 December 1961 President Kennedy traveled to New York to address the National Association of Manufacturers. This speech was important for the Kennedy administration if it was to gain business sector support for the Trade Expansion Act. This speech was important to the rhetoric of trade for its connection of U.S. economic welfare with the nation's political well-being. This was not a new presidential argument; what was new was the emphasis on conflict between the United States and the Soviet Union. Contrary to his address to Congress downplaying the urgency of the balance-of-payments position, Kennedy defined the expansion of trade as critical, not only to U.S. economic vitality, but also as the only peaceful means of combating the Soviet Union:

It's not an exaggeration to say that this endeavor of building a prosperous America, in a world of free and prosperous states, of making the most of our human and material resources and avoiding the harmful effects and fluctuations of inflation and recession, are of course matters of the greatest importance to us all.

And it's not an exaggeration to say that this endeavor proceeds under conditions today more fraught with peril than any in our history.

As communism continues its long-range drive to impose its way of life all around the world, our strongest desire is not unnaturally to seize the initiative, to get off the defensive, to do more than react to the Soviets. But while this is not an unreasonable urge, its concrete application is more difficult. In the military arena, the initiative rests with the aggressor—a role that we shun by nature and tradition—and our alliances are largely, therefore, defensive. In the paramilitary arenas of subversion, intimidation and insurrection, an open and peaceful society is again at a disadvantage.

But there is one area, in particular, where the initiative can and has been ours—an area of strategic importance in which we have the capacity for a still greater effort—and that is in the area of economic policy.[22]

Speaking to business, which was traditionally conservative, Kennedy emphasized his hard-line foreign policy and stressed that the United States could be the leader in the political Cold War through economic triumphs. Thus Kennedy elevated the issue of trade to a new plane. It was not just a matter of economic expediency; it was critical to the nation's very political freedom. Kennedy emphasized the importance of cooperating with the EEC to strike a blow for freedom for the developing countries:

This year's new long-range program [will] aid in the growth of the underdeveloped regions of the world, and the unaligned nations can bring us still further gains—not merely as a blow against communism but as a blow for freedom. Of equal if not greater importance is the stunning evolution of Western European economic unity from treaty to concrete reality. And it is the success of this still-growing moment which presents the West, at this time, with an historic opportunity to seize the initiative for its own self-interest and progress.

The Communist Bloc, largely self-contained and isolated, represents an economic power already by some standards larger than that of Western Europe and gaining to some degree on the United States. But the combined output and purchasing power of the United States and Western Europe is more than twice as great as that of the entire Sino-Soviet Bloc. Though we have only half as much population, and far less than half as much territory, our coordinated economic strength will represent a powerful force for the maintenance and growth of freedom.

But will our strength be combined and coordinated—or divided and self-defeating? Will we work together on problems of trade, payments, and monetary reserves—or will our mutual strength be splintered by a network of tariff walls, exchange controls, and the pursuit of narrow self-interest in unrelated if not outright hostile policies on aid, trade, procurement, interest rates and currency?[23]

Kennedy appealed to business, not on the basis of economic arguments involving the market success of free trade but, rather, on foreign policy grounds. Indeed, he asserted that to fail to support the expansion of free trade was to surrender to apparent immediate economic self-interest at the expense of national security. He continued to offer exports as the solution to the balance-of-payments problem and to suppress any tendency to control imports as an alternative solution.

Therefore, Kennedy outlined his administration's five-pronged strategy: first, increasing support to developing countries; second, implementing a government "Buy American" policy; third, promoting foreign investment in the United States; fourth, revising tax codes to promote domestic investment; and fifth, increasing exports, especially agricultural exports, to the European Economic Community. This plan of action signaled Kennedy's strategy to lower the balance-of-payments deficit. The president distinguished between the crisis of the Cold War, the role of the EEC, U.S. economic leadership, and the problem of the U.S. balance-of-payments deficit:

While exaggerated fears can be harmful, we could not inspire needed confidence abroad by feigning satisfaction with our international balance of payments position. In essence, that position reflects the burden of our responsibilities as the Free World's leader, the chief defender of freedom and the major source of capital investment around the world. There is cause for concern, in short, but I do not believe that there is cause for alarm.[24]

President Kennedy emphasized his firm commitment to export-oriented growth and reaffirmed his resistance to (inevitably ill-fated) protectionist measures:

For negative, shortsighted remedies will do more to weaken confidence in the dollar than strengthen it; and this Administration, therefore, during its term in office, and I repeat this, and make it a flat statement, has no intention of imposing exchange controls, devaluing the dollar, raising trade barriers, or choking off our economic recovery.

What we will do, and have been doing, is to take a series of positive steps to reduce our outpayments and to increase our receipts from abroad.[25]

Before this business audience, Kennedy stressed fiscal responsibility. His administration was limiting its own spending to resolve the balance-of-payments deficit:

In short, achieving a healthy equilibrium in our international accounts depends in part upon the cooperation of our Allies—in part upon action by the Congress—in part upon the self-discipline exercised by this Administration to its executive and budgetary policies (and I here repeat my intention to submit a balanced budget in January)—and in part upon you and other members of the business community. (Labor, too, has its responsibility for price stability, and I shall stress this tomorrow in addressing the AFL–CIO.) I recognize that your efforts will be governed in part by the kind of atmosphere the government can help to create. That is why we intend to submit our balanced budget. The government must not be demanding more from the savings of the country, nor draining more from the available supplies of credit, when the national interest demands a priority for productive, creative investment—not only to spur our growth at home but to make sure that we can sell, and sell effectively, in markets abroad.[26]

In this pitch for a united effort to revive the economy, Kennedy outlined the expected role of business in the recovery:

But your own responsibility is great—and there are three things in particular that you can do: be competitive, through lower costs and prices and better products and productivity. Be export-minded. In a very real sense, the British used to say they exported or died. We are going to meet our commitments. We've got to export. And we have to increase our exports, and however impressive it has been in the past, it must be better in the future for the security of this country.

And finally, be calm, in the sense of refraining from talk which really does not represent the facts, and which causes a concern about where we are going abroad. It is my hope that when we submit our balanced budget in January, that those who look at our fiscal situation from abroad and make their judgment, will recognize that we are in control, that we are moving ahead, and that the United States is a good bet.[27]

Once again, President Kennedy inflated the passage of the Trade Expansion Act to crisis dimensions and equated its failure with a threat to the nation's security. However, he also attempted to portray the U.S. economic position as strong: "All of us must share in this effort—for this in part, as I have said, is a part of the national security. And I don't want the United States pulling troops home because we're unable to meet our problems in other ways. But we can be calm because our basic international position is strong."[28]

This equivocation was the domestic equivalent of the domino theory. The United States was economically sound, yet failure to bolster the international economy would inevitably lead to defeat, both economically and politically. Kennedy explicitly defined the Trade Expansion Act as an integral weapon in the new arena of international economic competition:

The Reciprocal Trade Agreements Act expires in June of next year. It must not simply be renewed—it must be replaced. If the West is to take the initiative in the economic arena—if the United States is to keep pace with the revolutionary changes which are taking place throughout the world—if our exports are to retain and expand their position in the world market—then we need a new and bold instrument of American trade policy.[29]

President Kennedy defined security in the economic arena, for Europe as well as for the United States, as dependent on political security:

Our support—ever since the close of World War II—has been thrown behind greater European unity. For we recognized long ago that such unity would produce a Europe in which the ancient rivalries which resulted in two world wars, for us as well as for them, could rest in peace—a Europe in which the strength and the destiny of Germany would be inextricably tied with the West—and a Europe no longer dependent upon us, but on the contrary, strong enough to share in full partnership with us the responsibilities and initiatives of the Free World.[30]

However, while Kennedy was urging cooperation with Europe, he was also struggling under antiquated bargaining constraints. The European Common Market excluded American exports with high tariffs. Piecemeal negotiating was detrimental to U.S. economic interests: "For this is no longer a matter of local economic interest but of high national policy. We can no longer haggle over item-by-item reductions with our principal trading partners, but must adjust our trading tools to keep pace with world trading patterns—and the EEC cannot bargain effectively on an item-by-item basis."[31]

Kennedy did not reconcile the existence of economic competition with Europe with the need for political cooperation, yet he was careful to delineate between U.S. economic independence and the nation's political sovereignty:

I am proposing, in short, a new American trade initiative which will make it possible for the economic potential of these two great markets to be harnessed together in a team capable of pulling the full weight of our common military, economic and political aspirations. And I do not underrate at all the difficulties that we will have in developing this initiative. I am not proposing—nor is it necessary or desirable—that we join the Common Market, alter our concepts of political sovereignty, establish a "rich man's trading community," abandon our traditional most-favored-nations policy, create an Atlantic free trade area, or impair in any way our close economic ties with Canada, Japan and the rest of the Free World.[32]

Connecting U.S. economic prosperity with national security not only elevated the importance of successful passage of the Trade Expansion Act, it moved trade policy more closely into the realm of foreign policy, and thus more under the control of the president. While he reassured his business audience that the Trade Expansion Act would benefit the domestic economy, he also immediately shifted to the connection between the domestic economy and international markets:

But if we can obtain from the Congress, and successfully use in negotiations, sufficient bargaining power to lower Common Market restrictions against our goods, every segment of the American economy will benefit. There are relatively few members of the business community who do not or could not transport, distribute or process either exports or imports. There are millions of American workers whose jobs depend on the sale of our goods abroad—making industrial sewing machines, or trucks, or aircraft parts, or chemicals, or equipment for oil fields or mining or construction. They may produce lubricants or resin; they may dig coal or plant cotton. In fact, the average American farmer today depends on foreign markets to sell the crops grown on one out of every six acres he plants—in wheat, cotton, rice and tobacco, to name but a few examples. Our consumers, as mentioned, will benefit most of all.

But if American industry cannot increase its sales to the Common Market, and increase this nation's surplus of exports over imports, our international payments position and our commitments to the defense of freedom will be endangered.

If American businessmen cannot increase or even maintain their exports to the Common Market, they will surely step up their investment in new American-owned plants behind those tariff walls so they can compete on an equal basis—thereby taking capital away from us, as well as jobs from our own shores, and worsening still further our balance of payments position.

If American industry cannot increase its outlets to the Common Market, our own expansion will be stifled.[33]

Thus the national interest, if viewed apart from narrow, special interest concerns, benefited economically and politically from free trade. Kennedy argued that cooperation on an economic level, which he deemed comparable to cooperation on the military level, as exemplified by the North American Treaty Organization (NATO), was imperative:

Finally, let me add, if we cannot increase our sales abroad, we will diminish our stature in the Free World. Economic isolation and political leadership are wholly incompatible. The United Kingdom, faced with even more serious problems in her efforts to achieve both higher growth and reasonable balance of payments, is moving with boldness, welcoming, in the Prime Minister's words, "the brisk shower of competition." We cannot do less. For if the nations of the West can weld together on these problems a common program of action as extraordinary in economic history as NATO was unprecedented in military history, the long-range Communist aim of dividing and encircling us all is doomed to failure.[34]

Yet President Kennedy was not proposing an economic equivalent of NATO; the United States was not maneuvering to join the Common Market. Instead, in Kennedy's mindset, competition on the economic front between the West and the East was a new battleground in the Cold War:

In every sense of the word, therefore, Capitalism is on trial as we debate these issues. For many years in many lands, we have boasted of the virtues of the marketplace under free competitive enterprise, of America's ability to compete and sell, of the vitality of our system in keeping abreast with the times. Now the world will see whether we mean it or not—whether America will remain the foremost economic power in the world—or whether we will evacuate the field of power before a shot is fired, or go forth to meet new risks and tests of our ability.

The hour of decision has arrived. We cannot afford to "wait and see what happens," while the tide of events sweeps over and beyond us. We must use time as a tool, not a couch. We must carve our own destiny. This is what Americans have always done—and this, I have every confidence, is what we will continue to do in each new trial and opportunity that lies ahead.[35]

In Kennedy's rhetoric, passage of the Trade Expansion Act became the equivalent of a domestic crisis. This Cold War perspective combined with the perception of an active presidency to define action as a moral imperative. It was the United States versus the Soviet Union; the free world versus communism. It was not merely an issue of economic expediency or domestic prosperity. Indeed, while the support of business was essential to passage of the legislation, it was merely a foot soldier in a much larger war. Business should support Kennedy to increase profits through exporting, moreover, it must support Kennedy in order to preserve the free world.

Kennedy defined labor's role in the battle when, on 7 December 1961 (the following day), he addressed the convention of the American Federation of Labor and Congress of Industrial Organizations (AFL–CIO) in Miami. In speaking to business, Kennedy had stressed a balanced budget and restraint in government spending, but in speaking to labor, Kennedy stressed government spending on employment programs. Indeed, in the first segment of the speech, he listed six areas for government spending focusing on retraining.

As he did with business, Kennedy defined the expansion of trade as broader than pure economic interests, elevating it to the level of national security: "This country must maintain a favorable balance of trade or suffer severely from the point of view of our national security."[36] Kennedy continued to use the Common Market as the rationale for passing the Trade

Expansion Act: "Now the problems that we face have been intensified by the development of the Common Market. This is our best market for manufactured products."[37] Nonetheless, he emphasized throughout the connection to his immediate audience—labor and the union members' job concerns: "The purpose of this discussion is to increase employment. The purpose of this discussion is to strengthen the United States, and it is a matter which deserves our most profound attention. Are we going to export our goods and our crops or, are we going to export our capital? That's the question that we're now facing."[38]

However, while Kennedy defined the balance-of-payments deficit as an urgent problem, he did not deliver the original, more strident version of his speech, which read in part:

This is no time for timid answers or tired solutions. The European Economic Community is closing the history books on 2,000 years of divisive and self-centered trading philosophies. The new, once underdeveloped nations are seeking new outlets for their raw materials and new manufactures. No part of the world market is any longer ours by default. The competition grows keener. Our need to cover military and other expenditures abroad through greater dollar sales grows increasingly urgent. And the Soviet Union's economic and trade offensive grows greater every year.

When the current Reciprocal Trade Agreements Act expires in June, it must be replaced by a wholly new and bold approach, as revolutionary as the changes now going on in European commerce, as broad as our economic potential demand and deserves, and as challenging as the crisis and opportunity now facing American business and labor.

Whatever is required, we will make certain that no community suffers unduly from trade. For, on the contrary, America must trade—or suffer.

These are all, to be sure, new and untried concepts—but our challenges are new as well. America did not reach its present greatness by standing still, by refusing to try, to dare, to move ahead across uncharted seas. Now we must dare and do and move again—for the gain of the free spirit and for the profit of our souls.[39]

This strident version made the choice between mere revision of the trade act and complete renovation one of stark opposites. One path led to unmitigated catastrophe; the other, to economic nirvana. Revision would not suffice. This was no time "for timid answers or tired solutions." Nor was it a time for endless debate, as "the Soviet Union's economic and trade offensive grows greater every year." Certainly this was no time to rest: "Now we must dare and do and move again—for the gain of the free spirit and for the profit of our souls." By choosing the milder version of the speech, Kennedy underscored the cooperative nature of economic interdependence:

"The terms in which the choices open to the United States were presented in these preliminary sallies created some confusion as to what was meant by 'partnership' and whether it implied more than friendly competition. . . . [Thus,] President Kennedy made an effort to clarify his administration's intent."[40]

The following month, having addressed the key interest groups—business and labor—Kennedy began his private campaign to persuade Congress by sending a written message on 25 January 1962. Consistent with past presidents, Kennedy presented a stark contrast between free trade and protectionism by focusing on their opposing effects. In particular, free trade fostered competition and thus improved production, whereas protectionism sustained weak industries, leading to economic decline. However, Kennedy also made an argument that would become standard in the rhetoric of future presidents—that of the need for free, but fair, trade:

Once given a fair and equal opportunity to compete in overseas markets, and once subject to healthy competition from overseas manufacturers for our own markets, American management and labor will have additional reasons to maintain competitive costs and prices, modernize their plants, and increase their productivity. The discipline of the world marketplace is an excellent measure of efficiency and a force to stability. To try to shield American industry from the discipline of foreign competition would isolate our domestic price level from world prices, encourage domestic inflation, reduce our exports still further, and invite less desirable governmental solutions.[41]

Presidential rhetoric on trade contains the consistent line of argument that belief in free trade is equivalent to a belief in Americans' ability to successfully compete. President Kennedy argued from circumstances: a new situation made new legislation necessary if free trade policy was to continue to remain beneficial to U.S. interests. Therefore, Kennedy listed the five "fundamentally new and sweeping developments" making "obsolete our traditional trade policy."[42] These developments were, first, the growth of the European Common Market; second, growing pressures from the balance-of-payments position; third, the need to accelerate United States economic growth; fourth, countering a Communist aid and trade offensive; and fifth and most important, the need to open new markets in Japan and developing nations. To push for open markets for American exports, Kennedy was asking for new tariff-cutting authority. Therefore, he assured Congress that he would protect domestic interests and maintain "ample safeguards against injury to American industry and agriculture."[43] He initiated a new program of trade adjustment assistance to demonstrate his administration's commitment to labor. The president needed congressional support because he was dependent on the legislature for tariff-reducing authority; this was necessary to provide bargaining power for reducing the Common Market's external tariffs. In arguing for a reduction in tariffs, the president was relying on the traditional argument of the chief executive by supporting free trade on the basis of comparative advantage:

The major lines of argument advanced by the President for the trade legislation he was proposing cannot be said to have been new or startling. Rather, they represented the same basic approach to international trade—a liberal trade policy—which had underlain the trade agreements program since its inception in 1934. True, they stressed certain recent developments, such as the formation of a European Common Market, but such new reasons only added to the old grounds for concluding that it continued to be in the interest of the United States, and or the world, to press forward toward liberal trading policies.[44]

Kennedy used, but did not solely rely on, the traditional conservative argument for free trade, which involved the ability of the United States to compete rather than government intervention in the market. In using this argument, Kennedy stressed exports rather than the increased competition from imports. While it is imports that wave the red flag for the consumer-oriented public and special interest groups, exports strengthen support for free trade as well as buttressing the argument for a growth-oriented economy:

The fact that the "growth" argument—the export side of the free trade case—is stressed rather more than the "standards of living" argument—the import side—is not surprising. It has more general appeal since everyone is interested in more jobs and higher effective demand in an industrialized country. The argument for more efficient imports appeals only to the consumer-oriented segment of the economy and has little attraction for the less efficient domestic producer of articles competitive with such imports.[45]

President Kennedy's public and private persuasive campaigns were successful and culminated on 11 October, in passage of the Trade Expansion Act of 1962. Kennedy was given all the major powers he had requested. Congress did, however, impose safeguards to allow the monitoring of domestic interests.

[Congress also expressed] serious concern, more serious than ever before expressed, concerning the impact of the Common Market on American agricultural exports, and a strong desire that the President do everything that he can do reasonably to secure relief. This basically hortatory result should not be minimized, however, despite the fact that it may not result in withdrawal of concessions already granted. For it indicates to the President that he will have political as well as economic trouble at home unless in future negotiations he can secure commitments which will enable American agricultural exports to Europe to continue at close to historic levels.[46]

Congress enhanced the president's ability to protect American interests with three specific legislative revisions. First, it expanded his authority to negotiate tariff reductions in agreements with the European Common Market and other countries. Second, it changed the "safeguards against industry" provisions. Third (which was domestically and rhetorically most important), it added an "adjustment assistance" program. Having a domestic mechanism to relieve protectionist pressures assured foreign nations of America's resolve to avoid tariffs as a trade equalizer:

The importance and significance of adjustment assistance lies in the fact that, through its inclusion in the program, the United States has informed its trading partners, present and future, that it will make even more sparing use of tariff and quota relief in the future than it has in the past in those escape clause cases which merit relief. This should result in greater confidence on the part of the trading partners of the United States in the stability of the concessions which are negotiated, and this in turn should eventuate in greater exploitation by their business concerns of new market opportunities secured by such concessions. By the same token, this should enable the United States to request from its foreign trading partners similar restraint in "taking it out on imports" from the United States when the shoe is on the other foot, thereby assisting American export industries to make more vigorous efforts to capitalize on foreign market opportunities.[47]

Perhaps even more important, this provision allowed Congress and the president to assist firms and workers harmed by imports. In an increasingly interdependent economy, where free trade is economically advantageous, change will inevitably result in dislocations. Jobs are going to be lost in some industries and gained in others. Trade adjustment assistance provides a policy mechanism to accommodate displaced workers and thus a rhetorical mechanism to respond to protectionist pressures.

In addition to the adjustment assistance program, the 1962 Trade Expansion Act is notable for creating a special representative for trade policy. The trade representative has two primary duties: first, serving as chief representative for the United States in international negotiations, and second, chairing an interagency organization to aid the president in carrying out trade obligations. The creation of this office reflects the growing importance of trade policy to U.S. economic health. The coordination of trade policy also increases the potential for consistency and, thus, more effective presidential persuasion:

This, of course, does not mean that interagency differences, caused by differing interests, will vanish. It may not even mean that the Special Representative will in fact have decisive influence—that depends upon his relationship with the President, his performance and, as an interaction therefrom, his effective authority. But, at the least, the new structure provides a better opportunity for consistency, as well as continuing concern with the operation of the trade agreements program, a program which may be of even greater importance to the United States in the future than it has been in the past.[48]

Simply having a greater opportunity for consistency, though, does not make consistency altogether desirable. Indeed, while the Kennedy administration publically supported the expansion of trade, privately, import restrictions continued. On 2 May 1961, President Kennedy unveiled a program of assistance to the textile industry. He defined this decision as a product of the collective wisdom of a specially appointed committee as well as being in line with previous presidential commitments:

The problems of the textile industry are serious and deep-rooted. They have been the subject of investigation at least as far back as 1935, when a Cabinet committee was appointed by President Roosevelt to investigate the conditions in this industry. Most recently these problems were the subject of a special study by the Interdepartmental Committee headed by Secretary of Commerce Luther H. Hodges. I believe it is time for action.[49]

Kennedy relied on argument from circumstance: the conditions of the textile industry necessitated special treatment, especially given the number of workers affected and the already distressed nature of their communities. He also relied on his frequent trade argument connecting economic health with national security:

[The textile industry] is our second largest employer. Some 2 million workers are directly affected by conditions in the industry. There are another 2 million persons employed in furnishing requirements of the industry at its present level of production. Two years ago, the Office of Defense Mobilization testified that it was one of the industries essential to our national security. It is of vital importance in peacetime and it has a direct effect upon our total economy. All the studies have shown that unemployment in textile mills strikes hardest at those communities suffering most from depressed conditions.[50]

The argument that the national interest is dependent on textile production is probably the most transparent. The argument that the number of employees either working in textiles or affected by textiles means that the industry merits protection is the most specious. Protecting uncompetitive industries merely perpetuates economic inefficiency and the need for continued protection. Trade adjustment assistance—especially in the form of retraining dislocated workers—is a more economically sound method of intervening in the mechanisms of the free market. In effect, the administration was succumbing to protectionist pressures. Kennedy announced seven specific actions aiding the textile industry, including conducting research, offering depreciation allowances, providing financing for modernization, offsetting differences in production costs at home, doing so abroad, giving assistance to injured firms, and sponsoring an international textile conference. The impetus for these actions was not the economic health of the nation but, rather, the political health of the Kennedy administration. The action that would become increasing important in the internecine trade wars was the reliance on nontariff barriers (NTBs).

Voluntary restrictions on textiles were imposed in the Long-Term Cotton Textile Arrangement of 1 October 1962. Voluntary restrictions, which are quotas in practice but not in theory, skirt international law and, in effect, protect the industry in question from the competitive pressures of free trade: "The enormous volume of world trade in cotton textiles has been effectively removed from the scope of GATT prohibitions against both quantitative restrictions and discrimination."[51] The textile case is just one example of how, during the Kennedy Round, industries with political influence were "able to maintain tariff protection in the face of overall liberalization."[52] The Kennedy Round, named after President Kennedy for his role in passage of the Trade Expansion Act allowing U.S. participation in these international negotiations, had three primary agenda items: expanding trade with developing nations, reducing agricultural rates, and establishing rules for tariff cutting. The Kennedy Round, based on the most-favored-nation principle, dealt with all classes of products, agricultural and nonagricultural, and aimed at eliminating tariff and non-tariff barriers with the overall goal of trade liberalization.

Oil was another protected industry. When the administration imposed a "wafer-thin" increase in the quota on residential oil imports, the growing gap between Kennedy's free trade rhetoric and his protectionist actions was noted in the *Washington Post*: "This Administration has a way of using glowing rhetoric about free trade and then retreating in concrete instances into the foxholes of protectionism."[53] Kennedy, in his public campaign for the 1962 Trade Expansion Act, had inflated public expectations about the administration's commitment to free trade. True, politicians of all persuasions, at least on the national level, find it easy to support free trade in theory: "The run of politicians, from middle left to middle right, are very partial to liberal, internationalist rhetoric. Somehow or other, they find it better stuff for the making of speeches than conservative rhetoric. Possibly this is because it has a more hopeful sound and holds ambiguity better."[54]

However, in pushing for the Trade Expansion Act and in elevating both the prospects for free trade and the burdens of leadership, a return to a policy of select protectionist actions was most disappointing:

If this or any Administration can retreat in concrete instances from such rhetoric, as it most assuredly can, how much easier it is for it to fall back from a less advanced position! Advocates of freer trade would therefore be happier if the rhetoric, at least, remained incandescent, well knowing that to ask for surcease from hypocrisy in this world is equivalent to waiting for the pot of gold plus rainbow to fall in one's lap.[55]

President Kennedy's rhetoric in a 21 February news conference was more realistic. He acknowledged the need to balance requests for protection with a liberalized trade policy:

Well, we have discussed the problem of wool imports increasing from about 17 percent to 21 or 22 percent, and then the danger of going to 25 percent. This is a matter of concern.

On the other hand, the countries which are exporting to the United States are very anxious to maintain this market. I get periodic meetings from chicken growers who are anxious for us to prevent a free flow of chickens into Western Europe, and from other members of Congress who are anxious for us to prevent a free flow of textiles into the United States, and others who wish us not to limit the importation of oil, and others who wish us to encourage the exports of various other things into the market. It is quite difficult to get a balance, but that is what we are attempting to do. Governor [Christian A.] Herter [the chief trade negotiator] is working on it. We are attempting in this rather varied economy, with interests, some of which wish to encourage exports, some of which wish to diminish imports, we are attempting to get a fair balance.[56]

In the more mundane language of the press conference, Kennedy revealed the play between political interests and desirable economic policy. Special interests pressing for protection were politically powerful, especially as they were strengthened by the public's low interest in trade policy. Despite the public push for the Trade Expansion Act, the administration preferred political silence on trade. Kennedy began to use the language of fair trade in describing his administration's attempts to balance protectionist actions with a liberal free trade policy.

Most important, the direction of the administration was toward liberalized trade. Free trade rhetoric and protectionist actions are bound by the parameters of international frameworks and legislative grants of power. The Trade Expansion Act of 1962 was a major change in U.S. trade policy, as it expanded presidential authority to cut tariffs and simplified the procedures to do so. Tariff cuts averaged over 35 percent. However, this trend toward liberalized trade was met with resistance in the late 1960s as U.S. economic hegemony declined.

FREE TRADE BEYOND THE KENNEDY ADMINISTRATION

America's economic problems manifested themselves in a decline in the strength of the dollar. While the burden of attempting to balance the demands of the Great Society with financing the Vietnam War was at the heart of economic instability, the continued increase in the balance-of-payments deficit and the increasing flow of foreign imports remained a convenient scapegoat. Dozens of bills were introduced in Congress calling for increased quotas on specific items, including steel, textiles, and strawberries.[57] Nontariff barriers were indeed adversely affecting the dollar. President Lyndon Johnson issued a statement on 1 January 1968 decrying nontariff barriers and their role in the crisis affecting the U.S. dollar: "While the President's statement refrained from recommending new barriers to U.S. import trade and placed a substantial share of the blame for the crisis on inflation in the United States, he pointedly referred to the nontariff barriers of other countries and singled out for special attention their border tax adjustments."[58] Even though the Johnson administration continued in the tradition of favoring free trade, foreign nations were concerned that the executive branch would bow to protectionist pressures:

Throughout the second half of 1967 and all of 1968 the explosion of protectionist sentiment in the United States appeared capable at almost any moment of undoing the results of the Kennedy Round. Foreign governments were concerned with the sensitivity of the American democratic process; they were afraid that Congress would not, or could not, withstand the intense pressure being brought to bear on it by industries and labor unions seeking protection. They also showed that they took seriously the possibility of a move by the administration itself to correct the balance of payments deficit by direct action affecting the trade balance.[59]

The protectionist fervor was heightened by an administration-favored bill sent before Congress and intended to restore the expired tariff-cutting authority of the Trade Expansion Act. Importers and public interest groups supported the administration's position. The strength, however, lay with the opposition. The congressional Ways and Means Committee heard eight congressmen speak in favor of lowering tariffs and ninety-two speak against. Foreign nations were right to be concerned, as organized labor conditioned its support for free trade on foreign nations' reductions in nontariff barriers and increased labor standards. This support for a conditional free trade—based on an enforced reciprocity—was a break from labor's past:

Perhaps the most conspicuous shift in position was that of organized labor. In the past, specialized labor unions had often joined forces with their employers in demanding higher protection, but nationally organized labor had provided some of the most powerful backing for trade agreements legislation. In 1968, the spokesman for the AFL–CIO again supported the administration's trade proposals, but much of his testimony was devoted to insistence that the United States require of its trading partners, as a condition for the continuance of a liberal trade policy, prompt action to eliminate nontariff barriers and to raise their labor standards to a level closer to that of the United States. Equally urgent in his view was the need to curtail the export of American capital which has "cost American jobs, cut into American exports and added to imports."[60]

Labor had not yet come to vigorously oppose free trade, but these stirrings of opposition were harbingers of arguments to come. Not only did labor oppose the increasing use of nontariff barriers—by foreign nations—to exclude U.S. exports, but they also opposed investment by American companies in international markets:

In the United States, the internationalization of American enterprises has furnished domestically oriented business and organized labor with reason for genuine concern and with arguments for higher tariffs and import quotas. In the past, the contention that the United States cannot compete on even terms with low-wage producers abroad has been blunted both by the existence of a large U.S. trade surplus and by the demonstrable fact that U.S. labor, in combination with other productive factors available to it, was the most productive in the world. But, in 1968, advocates of import restrictions were able to point to the rapid decline in the U.S. trade surplus and to offer a superficially plausible explanation for it: capital, technology, and management were no longer a peculiarly American endowment. Through the medium of the multinational enterprise they had become as mobile as merchandise.[61]

International investment, which involves the movement of capital between enterprises both within a nation and between nations, is essential to
the free market. However, just as labor is hurt when industries falter
domestically, it also suffers as industries adjust to international markets.
The effect is even more damaging, however, on an international basis given
inherent feelings of nationalism. Jobs lost are seen as failures of domestic
enterprise, and hence, leadership. Compounding these nationalist tendencies are justifiable instances of international distortions of the free market.
Certainly, the United States has protected domestic industries in the name
of providing for the national defense and upholding free trade through fair
trade (often a veil for protecting politically powerful special interests).
However, other nations coordinate market functions via government planning and practice protectionism as a standard method of protecting domestic
industries, legitimating U.S. workers' claims of unfair trade. The primary
threat named by U.S. labor was low wages abroad.

To organized labor the new mobility of productive factors added up, quite simply,
to the export of American jobs; U.S. companies established production abroad
either in order to produce goods for foreign markets that could otherwise have been
exported from the United States or in order to satisfy American demand through
foreign low-wage production. The course proposed by the AFL–CIO was that "the
export of U.S. capital and its effect on international trade should be thoroughly
investigated, and appropriate supervision and necessary controls should be insti-
tuted by Government authorities." In this proposal it was implicit that if capital
controls were not imposed organized labor might turn to the support of trade
restrictions. "AFL–CIO support for the expansion of trade does not extend to the
promotion of private greed at public expense, or the undercutting of U.S. wages
and working conditions."[62]

Labor claimed that U.S. companies were not protecting the national
interest as they were failing to protect domestic jobs. Government intervention was the preferred solution, either through federal control of domestic
capital or through protectionism aimed at foreign nations. These interventionist proposals were consistent with government's parallel protection of
labor via, for example, fair labor laws and worker safety standards. However, government intervention was more directly at odds with the working
of the free market and Adam Smith capitalism. Moreover, these arguments
were economically dubious:

A favorite subject for dispute between internationally oriented businesses and their
critics is whether the exports generated by foreign investment—in the form of

shipments of capital goods and components and of merchandise to fill out the lines produced abroad—are greater or less than the exports that would have been possible had the capital stayed at home. But, to the policy maker, it should make little difference who has the better of this debate. The arguments for permitting the freest possible international trade in goods apply equally to the need for maximizing, within the limits imposed by time and space, the mobility of the factors of production. If governments should seriously interfere with that mobility, the result would be to stifle the growth in economic welfare that is otherwise possible.[63]

Free trade theory called for no market controls, despite the immediate harm to domestic workers and irregardless of the practices of other nations. Under the principle of comparative advantage, the best policy was to maximize free trade, including international investment. Rhetorically and politically, however, the best policy on trade was different, for it had to consider the consequences of adjustment. It was the perception of fairness that was critical to trade policy and the presumed increase in foreign trade barriers that heightened pressure for reciprocity and, if necessary, trade restrictions.

Constituency pressure for equivalent trade-restricting measures to match those of other nations was evident in the 1968 Ways and Means Committee hearings over the administration bill to restore tariff-cutting authority to the president, in which "the assumed escalation of foreign nontariff barriers colored the testimony of most public and congressional witnesses."[64] Democrat Congressman Peter W. Rodino of New Jersey stated:

It has come to my attention and to the attention of many other Members of the Congress that many of our trading partners abroad have already increased their border taxes to levels that more than offset the current reductions which they agreed to make at Geneva, so that the net effect, once again, is all give on our part and all take on their part. Their cost of entering the U.S. market is substantially reduced, but our cost of entering their market remains approximately the same. This tampering with border taxes cannot be ignored because it poses a serious threat to our already troublesome balance of payments and negates even the pretense of reciprocity in the Geneva agreements.[65]

The congressman was not refuting the merit of the principle of free trade, but rather castigating other nations for not practicing it. In response, he was suggesting reciprocal restrictions in the name of fair trade. It did not matter that fair trade is not a component of free trade theory. Fair trade is, rather, the most important argument in response to protectionist pressures. Nontariff barriers were the focus of congressional complaints, as noted in Congressman Thomas Curtis's (R–Mo.) testimony:

Many of us like to think that the decades since the war have been marked by a continuing movement toward freer world trade and payments. The Kennedy Round in this vision is seen by shortsighted persons as the crowning achievement of the drive forward for freer trade, but they have ignored the fact that as tariffs have been dismantled . . . [while] quotas, licenses, embargoes and other rigid and restrictive trade barriers have been created.[66]

There were two perceived forces in the deterioration of the U.S. trading position: first, the Kennedy Round negotiating reductions in trade barriers; and second, foreign nations' flouting of free trade standards via nontariff barriers. It was the latter that reverberated with nationalist sentiment:

Charges of massive cheating by America's trading partners found fertile soil. They helped explain the unsatisfactory performance of American industry in international competition. Even those who attributed the deterioration in the US trade balance to more fundamental changes in the structure of international trade found no logical difficulty in espousing at the same time a thesis that cast doubt on the equity of the Kennedy Round settlement.[67]

The tendency to blame foreign nations, admittedly justified for some trade-restricting measures, was enhanced by the European Economic Community actions that the EEC found necessary to coordinate economic functions, including trade barriers. The Johnson administration saw the utility in attacking foreign trade barriers and thus emphasizing foreign causes of U.S. economic troubles rather than the domestic burden of attempting to balance expenditures for the Great Society, the space program, and the war in Vietnam:

Much of the original impetus for the conviction that foreign governments were to blame, however, came from the Johnson administration itself. In order to explain the decline in the balance of payments without placing all the onus on the cost of distant adventures, terrestrial and extraterrestrial, it was natural for the administration to emphasize the responsibility of foreign governments. Also, in the fight against protectionism at home, it served the administration's immediate interest to demonstrate its vigilance by challenging the trespasses of other countries. In the complex of governmental measures affecting trade, shortcomings are never hard to find. But the efforts of the European Community to harmonize the internal taxes of the member states provided a particularly timely target.[68]

As regulations on trade-restricting measures were formalized via GATT, as symbolized by the Kennedy Round reductions, the use of nontariff barriers increased. Rhetorically, the executive branch has to balance its attacks on nontariff barriers by foreign nations with both its own trade—restricting measures—formal and informal—and the executive preference for free trade. The focus of international trade negotiations thus shifted. Not only did negotiators have to shift their focus from formal to informal trade barriers, they had to consider the increasing interdependence of economies as corporations increased foreign investment and production:

The fact that nontariff barriers are widely perceived as instruments that foreign countries are able to use to nullify tariff concessions makes it unlikely that any American administration could obtain authority from the Congress to engage in a major trade negotiation that did not promise to achieve their substantial curtailment. To this reason for predicting a qualitative change in the character of trade negotiations must be added another factor—the growth of the multinational corporation and the related revolution in the international mobility of production factors.[69]

Tariffs remained symbolically important in trade policy, but as the nature of the game changed, nontariff barriers and international investment became the new fodder in the trade policy wars. The best the administration could do in a battleground littered with the casualties of the 1962 Trade Expansion Act was achieve a stalemate. The ideal of the free trade policy was shattered by nontariff barriers and other extralegal barriers to trade. The Ways and Means Committee, under the guidance of Chairman Wilbur Mills (D–Ark.)—an ardent free trader and administration supporter—failed to rule on the administration's bill or on other quota bills before Congress adjourned for the 1968 elections. In this instance, Wills found it impossible to balance industry-specific demands for protection with the general goal of free trade.

Early the following year, Chairman Mills publicly expressed both his sympathy for the claims of the domestic textile industry for special protection and his attitude toward the general use of quotas: "The Congress always has trouble approving import quota legislation affecting a single industry. However sympathetic individual Representatives or Senators are to the textile import problem, there are other industries which are seeking the same form of relief and which also have supporters in the Congress. Thus, it appears difficult, if not impossible, to work out an import quota law for one industry and prevent its extension to the products of other industries."[70]

Liberals and Democrats, who were traditionally free traders, began to alter their rhetoric from a blanket espousal of free trade policy to support for free trade in the name of fair trade, which was seen as necessary as foreign competition had led to the perceived losses of American jobs, and nontariff barriers began to replace tariffs as the new weapons in the trade war. With the Richard Nixon administration, trade policy was about to undergo a significant shift.

THE 1970s: PROTECTIONIST PRESSURES AND INTERVENTION

The Proposed 1970 Trade Act

In the 1970s the U.S. trade picture worsened. There was increased exposure of the economy to trade as interdependence increased. There was also a relative decline in America's ability to compete with the rise of new competitors, particularly East Asia. There was an erosion of GATT as an effective arbitrator in the international arena. There was a worsening of stagflation in the United States and in Europe, with slow economic growth, high unemployment, and rapid price increases. Finally, floating exchange rates were misaligned, making imports inexpensive and exports expensive.

The Nixon administration attempted to ease the growing trade imbalance by engaging in public and private talks with Japan that focused on "voluntary" textile quotas. At the administration's request, Wilbur Mills initiated the 1970 act, which was intended to pressure Japan. In essence, Nixon was requesting the additional presidential powers necessary for him to pressure foreign nations into eliminating nontariff barriers. On 18 November 1969, Nixon sent a Special Message to Congress supporting new trade legislation. First and foremost, the president emphasized his continued commitment to the principle of free trade and his intent to proceed as a representative of the national interest: "For the past 35 years, the United States has pursued a policy of freer world trade. As a nation, we have recognized that competition cannot stop at the ocean's edge. We have determined that American trade policies must advance the national interest—which means they must respond to the whole of our interest, and not be a device to favor the narrow interest."[71]

Much as Kennedy had argued that changes in circumstances necessitated changes in trade policy, most notably an expansion of presidential powers, Nixon also argued from circumstance in asking for additional powers: "It is clear that the trade problems of the 1970's will differ significantly from those of the past. New developments in the rapidly evolving world economy will require new responses and new initiatives."[72] In describing such circumstances, Nixon asserted three interrelated causes—economic interdependence, foreign competition, and the disappearance of the United States trade surplus:

Three factors stand out that require us to continue modernizing our own trade policies:

First, world economic interdependence has become a fact. Reduction in tariffs and in transportation costs have internationalized the world communications network. The growth of multi-national corporations provides a dramatic example of this development.

Second, we must recognize that a number of foreign countries now compete fully with the United States in world markets. We have always welcomed such competition. It promotes the economic development of the entire world to the mutual benefit of all, including our own consumers. It provides an additional stimulus to our own industry, agriculture and labor force. At the same time, however, it requires us to insist on fair competition among all countries.

Third, the traditional surplus in the U.S. balance of trade has disappeared. This is largely due to our own internal inflation and is one more reason why we must bring that inflation under control.[73]

President Nixon's description of circumstances was relatively neutral. He did not provoke nationalist sentiment; indeed, he attributed the decline in the U.S. trade status to domestic causes, most notably inflation. He did not side with either labor or management but used neutral, passive language to state that the multinational corporations had grown, which was neither good nor bad in his parlance. Nixon adhered to the free trade ideal of the executive, with a (by-now familiar) insistence on fair trade. Consistent with his internationalist foreign policy, he argued for an economic leadership role for the United States rather than a retreat into economic isolationism: "In fact, the need to restore our trade surplus heightens the need for further movement toward freer trade. It requires us to persuade other nations to lower barriers which deny us fair access to their markets. An environment of freer trade will permit the widest possible scope for the genius of American industry and agriculture to respond to the competitive challenge of the 1970s."[74]

This was an intricate argument. It would seem that forcing other nations to practice free and fair trade would require retaliatory tariffs, yet Nixon was asking to reduce U.S. tariffs: "I recommend that the President be given authority to make modest reductions in U.S. tariffs."[75] As Hoover had argued making the case for the Smoot-Hawley legislation, Nixon argued that major trade-negotiating authority would remain with Congress. He was asking for additional powers only as necessary to adjust trading barriers to changes in circumstances: "This authority is not designed to be used for major tariff negotiations, but rather to make possible minor adjustments that individual circumstances from time to time require. . . . Lack of this authority exposes our exports to foreign retaliation."[76] Symbolic of his administration's intent to lower trade restrictions, including nontariff barriers, Nixon proposed eliminating the American Selling Price system, a tariff applicable to a small segment of U.S. imports: "The time has come for a serious and sustained effort to reduce non-tariff barriers to trade. These non-tariff barriers have become increasingly important with the decline in tariff protection and the growing interdependence of the world economy. Their elimination is vital to our efforts to increase U.S. exports. *As a first step in this direction, I propose today that the United States eliminate the American Selling Price system of customs valuation.*"[77]

Nixon made explicit the limited impact this adjustment would have on tariff levels, noting the more powerful symbolic importance of the action: "Although this system applies only to a very few American products— mainly benzenoid chemicals—it is viewed by our principal trading partners as a major symbol of American protectionism. Its removal will bring reciprocal reductions. . . . Because of the symbolic importance our trading partners attach to it, the American Selling Price system has itself become a major barrier to the removal of other barriers."[78]

Nixon was emphasizing the rhetorical importance of actions in trade policy. He asked Congress for a specific declaration of support: "I would welcome a clear statement of Congressional intent with regard to non-tariff barriers to assist in our efforts to obtain reciprocal lowering of such barriers."[79] Furthermore, he was careful to define the parameters of his actions as within the control of Congress:

It is not my intention to use such a declaration as a "blank check." On the contrary, I pledge to maintain close consultation with the Congress during the course of any such negotiations, to keep the Congress fully informed on problems and progress, and to submit for Congressional consideration any agreements which would require new legislation. The purpose of seeking such an advance declaration is not to bypass Congress, but to strengthen our negotiating position.

In fact, it is precisely because ours is a system in which the Executive cannot commit the Legislative Branch that a general declaration of legislative intent would be important to those with whom we must negotiate.[80]

Not only did Nixon continue to stress fair trade to alleviate congressional concerns about constituency pressure, he also emphasized new programs in the legislation to allow for improved assistance for dislocated workers:

Freer trade brings benefits to the entire community, but it can also causes hardship for parts of the community. The price of a trade policy from which we all receive benefits must not fall unfairly on the few—whether on particular industries, on individual firms or on groups of workers. As we have long recognized, there should be prompt and effective means of helping those faced with adversity because of increased imports.

The Trade Act of 1969 provides significant improvements in the means by which U.S. industry, firms, and workers can receive assistance from their government to meet injury truly caused by imports.[81]

The arguments Nixon was making were consistent with the cry-and-sigh syndrome. As president, he would relieve Congress of constituent pressure while assuring members that he would protect workers in affected industries. Congress could press for fair trade while relinquishing the burden of action to the president. This explained the emphasis on fair trade and the new prominence given to adjustment assistance programs. Nixon recognized that current assistance provisions were inadequate: "The assistance programs provided in the Trade Expansion Act of 1962 have simply not worked. The escape clause provisions of the 1962 Act have proved so stringent, so rigid, and so technical that in not a single case has the Tariff Commission been able to justify a recommendation for relief."[82]

However, continuing to support free trade also meant acknowledging the temporary nature of such import relief: "While making these escape clause adjustments more readily obtainable, however, we must ensure that they remain what they are intended to be: temporary relief measures, not permanent features of the tariff landscape. An industry provided with temporary escape-clause relief must assume responsibility for improving its competitive position."[83]

There was no economically adequate argument to justify continued protection of textiles—a measure politically motivated. Nixon merely stressed fair trade in his argument from circumstance:

The textile import problem, of course, is a special circumstance that requires special measures. We are now trying to persuade other countries to limit their textile shipments to the United States. In doing so, however, we are trying to work out with our trading partners a reasonable solution which will allow both domestic and foreign producers to share equitably in the development of the U.S. market. Such measures should not be misconstrued, nor should they be allowed to turn us away from the basic direction of our progress toward freer exchange.[84]

Textiles were a political aberration in United States trade policy. Therefore, they merely warranted an aside in an otherwise consistent speech. Nixon repeatedly linked free trade with fair trade: "By nature and by definition, trade is a two-way street. We must make every effort to ensure that American products are allowed to compete in world markets on equitable terms. These efforts will be more successful if we have the means to take effective action when confronted with illegal or unjust restrictions on American exports."[85]

Given new economic circumstances, Nixon attacked the adequacy and continued reliance on the old dualism of liberalism (or free trade) versus protectionism:

Intense international competition, new and growing markets, changes in cost levels, technological developments in both agriculture and industry, and large-scale exports of capital are having profound and continuing effects on international production and trade patterns. We can no longer afford to think of our trade policies in the old, simple terms of liberalism vs. protectionism. Rather, we must learn to treat investment, production, employment and trade as interrelated and interdependent.[86]

Economic leadership was a vital and necessary aspect of U.S. leadership in world affairs:

By expanding world markets, our trade policies have speeded the pace of our own economic progress and aided the development of others. As we look to the future, we must seek a continued expansion of world trade, even as we also seek the dismantling of those other barriers—political, social and ideological—that have stood in the way of a freer exchange of people and ideas, as well as of goods and technology.

Our goal is an open world. Trade is one of the doors to that open world. Its continued expansion requires that others move with us, and that we achieve reciprocity in fact as well as in spirit.[87]

While Nixon did not rhetorically rely on trade as an index of economic and political alliances in the Cold War as much as had Kennedy, he did continue to link economic and political freedom.

However, in light of continued constituency pressure for fair trade, Nixon's request for additional powers to lower tariffs was not successful. The 1970 Trade Act did not pass Congress, which transformed the proposed bill into "the most protectionist trade act since the depression of the

1930's."[88] Congress demanded increased reciprocity—in other words, increases rather than decreases in tariffs. The proposed trade act stood as a symbol of opposition to lower tariffs.

Although Congress did not provide Nixon with increased authority to reduce tariffs, its failure to pass the bill indirectly boosted the president's power in negotiations to demand fairer trade via the cry-and-sigh syndrome: "Congress used this trade bill as a signal to the Executive Branch, the Japanese, and the Tariff Commission. (The Commission got the message first and began processing petitions more quickly and with more evenhandedness; that is, it did not deny every petition. Japan also reduced some of its nontariff barriers and subsequently agreed to limit its textile exports.)"[89] In fact, since the administration had initiated the bill to pressure Japan, even though it did not pass, it did achieve its desired purpose.

The Divorce of the Dollar from the Gold Standard

The U.S. trade picture continued to worsen. Protectionist pressures continued. The Nixon administration acted. On 15 August 1971, Nixon took steps to reduce the value of the dollar by selling gold reserves, encouraging other nations to raise the value of their currencies, and adding a temporary 10 percent surcharge to imports. In his "Address to the Nation Outlining a New Economic Policy," given on 15 August, Nixon defined these actions as necessary to pursuing peacetime prosperity: "Prosperity without war requires action on three fronts: We must create more and better jobs; we must stop the rise in the cost of living; we must protect the dollar from the attacks of international money speculators."[90]

Nixon was waging an economic war, using military language to justify his actions as commander in chief. In announcing his actions to freeze prices and wages and divorce the dollar from the gold standard, Nixon continued with the military metaphor:

I am today ordering a freeze on all prices and wages throughout the United States for a period of 90 days. . . . Let me emphasize two characteristics of this action: First, it is temporary. To put the strong, vigorous American economy into a permanent straitjacket would lock in unfairness; it would stifle the expansion of our free enterprise system. And second, while the wage-price freeze will be backed by Government sanctions, if necessary, it will not be accompanied by the establishment of a huge price control bureaucracy. I am relying on the *voluntary* cooperation of all Americans—each one of you: workers, employers, consumers—to make this freeze work.[91]

The temporary nature of the measures allowed Nixon to reconcile intervention with continued belief in the free market. The voluntary nature of the actions, however, was more problematic. When appealing to patriotism in this economic war, the government's threat of sanctions nullified the spirit of cooperation. In addition, these threats of government sanctions were directed at Nixon's own supporters—his very own troops. In effect, he was emphasizing the penalties for desertion rather than the benefits of enlistment. The asset to be defended in this case was not ground, but rather the nation's currency:

We must *protect* the position of the American dollar as a pillar of monetary stability around the world. The *strength* of a nation's currency is based on the strength of that nation's economy—and the American economy is by far the strongest in the world. Accordingly, I have directed the Secretary of the Treasury to take the action necessary to *defend* the dollar against the speculators.

I have directed [Treasury] Secretary [John] Connally to suspend temporarily the convertibility of the dollar into gold or other reserve assets, except in amounts and conditions determined to be in the interest of monetary stability and in the best interests of the United States.[92]

Nixon highlighted his metaphoric terms of war. This was the rhetoric of an intermestic crisis, for when it came down to the interests of the United States versus those of foreign nations, the president left no doubt which side prevailed.

Nixon was enlisting Americans in his fight for fair trade. Using a metaphor of war helped in justifying his drastic action of divorcing the dollar from the gold standard, yet while elevating the situation to that of a crisis, the president then stepped back to reassure his citizens that these actions would not wreak undue havoc on the American economy. His address suddenly turned to the parlance of everyday life:

Now, what is this action—which is very technical—what does it mean for you? Let me lay to rest the bugaboo of what is called devaluation.

If you want to buy a foreign car or take a trip abroad, market conditions may cause the dollar to buy slightly less. But if you are among the overwhelming majority of Americans who buy American-made products in America, your dollar will be worth just as much tomorrow as it is today.

The effect of this action, in other words, will be to stabilize the dollar.[93]

Instead of the commander in chief, Nixon now was depicted as a teacher to the nation—yet the patriotic appeal remained. The majority of Americans—who bought domestic goods and rarely traveled abroad—would not be adversely affected. Nixon made explicit his priority of domestic over foreign interests: "Now, this action will not win us any friends among the international money traders. But our primary concern is with the American workers, and with fair competition around the world."[94] His attack on the international money traders reflected his distaste for the economic elite, which was often manifested domestically in his dislike of the "Eastern establishment."

However, as president, Nixon was responsible for integrating the nation into an interdependent economy. What is most remarkable was his change in priorities: from the American economic and political leadership necessary to triumph in the Cold War in his push for the 1970 Trade Act, to subsequently, his almost total emphasis on domestic interests fighting for fairness in free and fair trade. However, he did not neglect the international arena, assuring foreign nations that the United States remained committed to an interdependent world economy:

To our friends abroad, including the many responsible members of the international banking community who are dedicated to stability and the flow of trade, I give this assurance: The United States has always been, and will continue to be, a forward-looking and trustworthy trading partner. In full cooperation with the International Monetary Fund and those who trade with us, we will press for the necessary reforms to set up an urgently needed new international monetary system. Stability and equal treatment [are] in everybody's best interest. I am determined that the American dollar must never again be a hostage in the hands of international speculators.[95]

Nixon reinforced the nation's commitment to the ideal of free trade and international economic institutions, despite the administration's imposition of a 10 percent import surcharge. Nixon defined this measure as necessary for the protection of American jobs and presented the only alternative—import controls—as a far worse option: "I am taking one further step to protect the dollar, to improve our balance of payments, and to increase jobs for Americans. As a temporary measure, I am today imposing an additional tax of 10 percent on goods imported into the United States. This is a better solution for international trade than direct controls on the amount of imports."[96]

Nixon defined this action as temporary and defensive: it was being imposed only due to unfair trading practices of other nations. Contrary to his 1969 stance, in which he attributed the decline in the U.S. balance of payments to internal inflation, by 1971 Nixon—who now was being held more responsible for the economy and facing re-election—attributed the decline in the U.S. trading position to the unfair trading practices of foreign nations. The United States continued to remain true to the principle of free trade but would practice fair trade until foreign nations reciprocated:

This import tax is a temporary action. It isn't directed against any other country. It is an action to make certain that American products will not be at a disadvantage because of unfair exchange rates. When the unfair treatment is ended, the import tax will end as well.

As a result of these actions, the products of American labor will be more competitive, and the unfair edge that some of our foreign competition has will be removed. This is a major reason our trade balance has eroded over the past 15 years.[97]

Not only did Nixon have to reconcile economic intervention with the principle of free trade, he also had to reconcile interference in the market with the Republican ideal of a limited government. Thus, in conclusion, Nixon used the familiar presidential argument of faith in the ability of the American competitive spirit to triumph: "But government, with all of its powers, does not hold the key to the success of a people. That key, my fellow Americans, is in your hands. A nation, like a person, has to have a certain inner drive in order to succeed. In economic affairs, that inner drive is called the competitive spirit."[98]

Nixon foreshadowed President Jimmy Carter's infamous "malaise speech" when he cautioned the American people of the consequences of sloth—a mortal enemy when opposed to Nixon's devotion to hard work and the self-made man: "Whether this Nation stays number one in the world's economy or resigns itself to second, third, or fourth place; whether we as a people have faith in ourselves, or lose that faith; whether we hold fast to the strength that makes peace and freedom possible in this world, or lose our grip—all that depends on you, on your competitive spirit, your sense of personal destiny, your pride in your country and in yourself."[99]

President Nixon also foreshadowed the growing importance of international economic competition as military competition declined, even prior to the end of the Cold War: "We can be certain of this: As the threat of war recedes, the challenge of peaceful competition in the world will greatly increase."[100] Nixon thus progressed to contrasting the increasingly important alternatives of interdependence versus isolationism: "We welcome competition, because America is at her greatest when she is called on to compete. As there always have been in our history, there will be voices urging us to shrink from that challenge of competition, to build a protective wall around ourselves, to crawl into a shell as the rest of the world moves ahead."[101]

Nixon rejected isolationism by harking back to previous false alarms of defeatism:

Two hundred years ago a man wrote in his diary these words: "Many thinking people believe America has seen its best days." That was written in 1775, just before the American Revolution—the dawn of the most exciting era in the history of man. And today we hear the echoes of those voices, preaching a gospel of gloom and defeat, saying the same thing: "We have seen our best days."

I say, let Americans reply: "Our best days lie ahead."[102]

As did previous presidents, Nixon grounded a successful trade policy in faith in America's ability to compete, selling free trade as belief in the American spirit of the past, present, and future.

The Trade Act of 1974

The 1970 Legislative Reorganization Act increased congressional policy-making autonomy, yet Congress remained reluctant to retrieve its authority in trade policy as decisions on individual tariffs continued to contain more political landmines than benefits. Simultaneously, economic circumstances enhanced the president's authority in trade as political circumstances diminished his powers in other policy areas. Worldwide inflation in 1973 led to import liberalization. Nixon's devaluation of the dollar, as detailed in the Bretton Woods Agreement, resulted in the floating exchange rate system. There was no international set of rules governing exchange market interventions. Therefore, it was easier for countries to manipulate exchange rates to their own advantage.

In his 1974 State of the Union Address, Nixon continued to support a policy of free, but fair, trade. First, he emphasized the importance of exports to both producers and consumers: "A vigorous international trade is vital to the American economy. Jobs for American workers depend on our ability to develop foreign markets. Moreover, American consumers deserve access to foreign-made products that might be less expensive, or more interesting, or unavailable in the United States."[103]

Second, Nixon repeated his 1970 call for increased negotiating authority to press foreign nations to lower trade barriers:

If trade is to be advantageous over the long run, it must be conducted on a basis which is fair to all participants.

There are still many unnecessary barriers to trade which need to be lowered or removed. While improvements have been made in this situation during the last 10 years, we need now to build on this progress and to negotiate for more open access

both to markets and supplies. This is why I call upon the Congress with special
urgency to complete action on my proposed Trade Reform Act, in order to provide
the authority we will need to negotiate effectively for reductions in barriers to trade,
to improve the trading system, and to manage trade problems at home more
effectively.[104]

While asking for more powers, Nixon rejected proposed legislative
conditions on trade in the form of the Jackson-Vanik amendment, which
tied most favored nation status, with favorable trading conditions for the
Soviet Union to liberalized emigration policies for Soviet Jews. Nixon
correctly countered that the emigration of Soviet Jews was already increasing because of private negotiations between the United States and the Soviet
Union. Moreover, the amendment impinged upon the administration's bargaining powers:

As the Senate considers this legislation, I would draw its attention particularly to
provisions added in the House which would seriously impede our efforts to achieve
more harmonious international relationships. These provisions would effectively
prevent both the extension of nondiscriminatory tariff treatment and of credits to
certain Communist countries unless they followed a policy which allowed unrestricted emigration. I am convinced that such a prohibition would only make more
difficult the kind of cooperative effort between the United States and other governments which is necessary if we are to work together for peace in the Middle East
and throughout the world.[105]

President Nixon made explicit the connection between economic and
political policies and he continued to argue from circumstance. The United
States was no longer the undisputed economic leader, and cooperation was
therefore becoming more vital: "As we turn from an era of confrontation to
one of cooperation, trade and commerce become more important. We have
moved from a position of virtual economic hegemony in the world to a new
role in a more interdependent world economy. We must create an equitable
and efficient system of integrating our own economy with that of the rest
of the world."[106]

President Nixon presented the 1974 Trade Reform Act as vital to modernizing the international trading order: "Prompt passage of the pending
Trade Reform Act is essential to achieving the goal of a less restrictive and
more equitable international economic system. In addition, we must move
forward with the current negotiations to reform the international payments
system under the auspices of the International Monetary Fund, reforms

which will markedly increase the opportunities for nations to trade and invest profitably."[107]

Nixon conceded that the United States was no longer the presumed economic leader—that is, not without competition. He allowed that international economic institutions needed to be modernized to promote and enforce fair trade. Nonetheless, he continued to position the United States as an economic benefactor:

We must also strengthen our resolve as the world's most prosperous nation to help less fortunate countries. In the world of today, no nation will be fully secure or prosperous until all nations are. . . . Strengthening international economic cooperation is essential to our quest for peace. Expansion of peaceful trade relationships helps bind together the peoples of the world. We have already made considerable progress toward international monetary reform, progress which has helped bring about dramatic improvement in our balance of payments. The Trade Reform Act, now before the Congress, would authorize U.S. participation in a new round of international discussions to reduce trade barriers. Failure to enact this message in a responsible form could result in a wave of trade protectionism that would undermine the economic well-being of all nations. I urge the Congress to approve it.[108]

Nixon also relied on the domino theory in trade policy: moving toward protectionism—in this case, by refusing to approve the Trade Act—would result in a wave of protectionist measures. In 1974, the Trade Reform Act did pass Congress. The executive and legislative branches compromised. Cooperation was essential as the trade balance continued to increase. In return for its support, Congress received assurances that the administration would enforce fair trade:

The bill was a compromise between congressional and presidential views of the best policy and process to ensure the continued liberalization of the international trading system. Congress argued successfully for more automatic and generous adjustment assistance, more flexible and equitable criteria for import relief, and more participation and power in the negotiating process for itself and the general public. The executive insisted on maximum flexibility to negotiate and administer the law but reached compromise on both. On the key issue of how to obtain congressional approval of future agreements on nontariff barriers, both branches forged an innovative compromise that gave Congress the power to accept the agreement affirmatively but clear deadlines for it to act.[109]

The burden of decision, of meshing legitimate action against unfair trade with the continued pursuance of free trade, remained with the president: "The Trade Act of 1974, like its predecessors, succeeded in channeling the pressure for industry-specific remedies into general principles, which would allow an adjudicatory body, the International Trade Commission, to determine the legitimacy of the complaint. The ultimate decision on relief rested with the President."[110] Congress continued to delegate trade authority to the president, preferring the option of a rhetorical outlet for protectionist pressures without the adjoining political burden of individual decisions on tariffs.

SUMMARY OF ECONOMIC ARGUMENTS

Even as the U.S. economy underwent dramatic changes, American presidents remained committed to the principle of free trade. However, the conditions set in Ricardo's theory of comparative advantage, which held that free trade was mutually profitable only in the presence of specialization, equilibrium in exchange rates, and a competitive marketplace, were increasingly violated in world markets. Exchange rate differentials have recently plagued the United States. The most severe bouts of protection followed periods of overinflation of the dollar: in the early 1970s, 1976–1977, and 1983.

The most consistent and significant cause of protectionist actions, however, has been the influence of special interest groups on the political process. Special interest groups, also known as distributive coalitions, often prevent competitive markets even in the absence of government intervention.[111] The abiding influence of special interest groups promoting protection has forced proponents of free trade to ground their support for unfettered markets in the name of fair trade.

Based on economic theory alone, free trade would be the most advantageous policy for the United States regardless of the practices of other nations. Economic decisions, however, cannot be divorced from political circumstances. Therefore, the rhetoric of trade cannot be examined apart from economic and political developments. The political locus for trade policy has shifted from the congressional arena, where it involves legislative decisions; to the executive branch, where it involves administration decisions, executive orders, and agreements; to the international arena, where it involves GATT settlements or negotiated agreements (involving the executive and legislative branches).[112] However, with the erosion of GATT and the rise of nontariff barriers, the executive branch has returned to prominence in the trade arena. Because of this very division of power, the executive, legislative, and even judicial branches rely on signals—in other words, on rhetorical power—to enhance their own power with the public, and hence within the government. Thus, the politics of trade cannot be adequately assessed without an understanding of the inherent rhetorical nature of trade policy:

To understand trade policy and Congress' role in making it, one also needs to distinguish among policies and between policies and "signals." To paraphrase an Orwellian quip, all policies may be equal, but some are clearly more equal than others. Some of the confusion about U.S. trade policy and whether it is liberal or protectionist—open or closing—is based on a failure to distinguish between a major trade law and the introduction of a trade bill, between a decision by the International Trade Commission (ITC) and a petition filed there, between an executive order by the president and a comment made by an under secretary of commerce in the course of negotiating with a Japanese delegation.[113]

Rhetorical signaling occurs both internationally and domestically, but the symbolic nature of trade policy is especially relevant in understanding the dynamics of policy making between the executive and legislative branches:

The cries of protectionism are often provoked by congressional bills, resolutions, speeches, or hearings, but these are often intended more as signals to the executive branch, foreign governments, or local constituents than as policy; they are not commitments. . . . Therefore, trade laws and agreements are the most important items of trade policy; congressional resolutions, bills, speeches, and hearings are more useful in explaining the process and the politics than the policy.[114]

Legislation is the centerpiece of U.S. trade policy. It is the principle rule-setting mechanism for both domestic policy and international negotiations and the organizing principle driving presidential rhetoric on trade. Domestically, the executive branch has increasingly relied on the courts to allocate the burdens and benefits of economic change, thereby avoiding the negative redistributory effects of trade policy. The extent to which the president has advocated free trade has varied with each occupant of the office. Theodore Roosevelt and Woodrow Wilson worked for tariff reform, but "refrained from enlisting public strategies."[115] Franklin Roosevelt, Truman, Kennedy, and Nixon all aggressively pushed for free trade. Carter did not view protectionist legislation as an important foreign policy tool and therefore neglected trade policy, thus overlooking an important weapon (especially with the developing countries) in the executive's foreign policy arsenal.[116]

Economic decisions have political consequences, yet politicians attribute problems to economic forces and promise to get the economy moving again as if it were a distinct entity. As a result, the political dimensions of economic policies have been systematically obscured.[117] Because there is a political risk for politicians advancing policies promoting adjustment over protection, presidents have stressed improvements in adjustment assistance programs.

Public opinion on trade policy depends on the stratum of the public being examined. Historically, informed public opinion has shifted from favoring protectionism to favoring free trade, yet the portion of the public that is activated, and thus vocal, tends to consistently favor protection, as reflected in the semantics of trade policy (which in turn are based on the often erroneous assumptions of politicians):

They may, for example, respond to what they believe is a pervasive prejudice of the electorate against imports. Or, even if there is not reason to believe that the population considers imports per se to be evil or unpatriotic, they may act on the assumption that it will disapprove of any increase in imports that is not directly compensated by an equal increase in exports. But such explanations do not fit very closely with the trend in public opinion in the United States since the end of World War II.[118]

In the 1930s, lobbyists for the Smoot-Hawley Act prefaced statements with their support for protectionism, yet by the 1950s, the American Tariff League had tellingly changed its name to the Trade Relations Council.[119] The labels presidents use to obscure protectionist legislation are equally revealing: "Recent American administrations have found it desirable to avoid the unpleasant words 'restriction' or 'protection' to characterize their occasional concessions to business pressures; in official pronouncements, for example, the framework within which petroleum imports are curtailed is almost invariably referred to as the 'Oil Import Program.' "[120]

This disparity between rhetoric and policy is not new to contemporary American policy makers, but it became especially evident as the United States lost its economic hegemony and domestic economics increasingly influenced trade policy. A prime symbol of the U.S. decline in international trade politics was the trade deficit. From 1894 through 1970, the United States had a positive balance in trade, and yet from 1971 through the present, except for a single period of two years, the United States has had a negative trade deficit. The increase in foreign-owned firms has contributed to the deficit; such firms have become much more prevalent because of improved transportation, which decreases the cost of sending goods around the world;

technological improvements, which allow vast economies of scale; and the tastes of today's consumers, which have become more homogeneous.[121] The decline in the U.S. trading position was also caused by the complacency of domestic businesses following their postwar successes and their failure to adapt to the demands of an interdependent economy. Some companies depended on low-skilled operations in poorer areas and relied on Japan for high-technology components. Other companies focused on mergers and acquisitions, relied on protection to remain competitive, or depended on defense contracts. By 1980, 70 percent of U.S. goods were competing with foreign products.[122]

The trade deficit had several ramifications for U.S. trade policy. First, the deficit undercut the argument that the United States could afford to absorb the domestic costs of promoting free trade internationally. Second, it increased political receptivity to labor's claims of unfair competition. Third, American negotiators were put on the defensive.[123] While a negative trade deficit was actually an indication of a strong economy, it was a potent symbol for protectionist forces.[124]

In the 1980s, existing trade laws and bureaucratic decisions played a minor role in the direction of U.S. trade policy. Nonetheless, trade laws and practices, as embodied by tariffs, remained potent rhetorically: "It might well be argued that today the tariff is no longer a major element in the conduct of U.S. foreign trade. Nonetheless, it clearly remains the symbol of protection to both its friends and enemies."[125] However, while trade policy has swung from protectionism to free trade and the tariff has shifted from being an accepted practice to a questionable economic tool, the arguments in trade policy have remained amazingly static: "In a sense there are today almost no truly new arguments, though the weight and salience of them have shifted."[126]

By the 1980s voluntary export restraints (negotiated privately) and orderly market agreements (explicit bilateral agreements) took precedence over the multilateral negotiations of GATT and public tariffs.[127] With the erosion of GATT and the subsequent increase in nontariff barriers, the United States lost an important rhetorical argument for free trade—the need to "play by the rules."[128] Thus the debate over trade in the 1980s was not between free trade and protection but rather over the appropriate degree of protection in an environment in which fair trade had become an accepted reality: "The debate will not be a theoretical one between free trade and protection but about the degree and type of government intervention which is internationally acceptable and how to minimize distortions which result from that intervention."[129]

The executive branch continued its dominance in trade policy in the 1980s. A decentralized Congress, lacking the power of the old committees, was unable to resist specific import restrictions. Trade policy was thus more dependent on executive policy commitment and leadership skills—hence, the rhetorical powers of the president. Presidential decision making, as bound by congressional parameters, remained at the forefront in trade policy. With an increasingly interdependent world economy and the decline in the U.S. economic hegemony, chances for presidential success in trade policy have considerably decreased. At the same time, expectations for presidential action have increased as the trade deficit has become increasingly burdensome. Herein lies the dilemma for presidential rhetoric on trade: the necessity of balancing increased expectations with diminishing chances for success.

NOTES

1. John W. Evans, *The Kennedy Round in American Trade Policy* (Cambridge: Harvard University Press, 1971), 43.

2. John M. Dobson, *Two Centuries of Tariffs* (Washington, D.C.: United States International Trade Commission, 1976), 45–82.

3. Stephen D. Cohen, *The Making of United States Economic Policy*, 2nd ed. (New York: Praeger, 1981), xvi.

4. Stanley D. Metzger, *Trade Agreements and the Kennedy Round* (Fairfax, Va.: Corner Publications, 1964), 17–18.

5. Evans, *The Kennedy Round*, 137.

6. Ibid., 138–139.

7. See ibid., 134–135.

8. All quotes from Kennedy's 6 February 1961 "Special Message to the Congress on Gold and the Balance of Payment Deficit" are from Kennedy, *Public Papers 1961*, 58–60.

9. Evans, *The Kennedy Round*, 139.

10. Raymond Bauer, Ithiel de Sola Pool, and Lewis Anthony Dexter, *American Business and Public Policy* (Chicago: Aldine-Atherton, 1972), 96.

11. Ibid.

12. See ibid., 86.

13. Ibid., 94.

14. Ibid., 315.

15. Ibid., 103–104.

16. See Evans, *The Kennedy Round*, 139–141.

17. Ibid.

18. Ibid.

19. Ibid.

20. Ibid.

21. Ibid.

22. Kennedy, *Public Papers 1961*, 775.

23. Ibid.

24. Ibid., 776–777.

25. Ibid.

26. Ibid., 780–781.

27. Ibid.

28. Ibid.

29. Ibid., 781.

30. Ibid., 781–782.

31. Ibid.

32. Ibid.

33. Ibid., 783.

34. Ibid., 784.

35. Ibid.

36. Ibid., 790.

37. Ibid., 791.

38. Ibid.

39. Ibid.

40. Metzger, *Trade Agreements*, 94.

41. Ibid.

42. Ibid., 1.

43. Ibid.

44. Ibid., 7–10.

45. Ibid., 8.

46. Ibid., 36–37.

47. Ibid., 79–80.

48. Ibid., 92.

49. Kennedy, *Public Papers 1961*, 345–346.

50. Ibid.

51. Evans, *The Kennedy Round*, 53.

52. Howard P. Marvel and Edward J. Ray, "The Kennedy Round: Evidence on the Regulation of International Trade in the United States," *American Economic Review*, 73 (March 1983): 190.

53. Metzger, *Trade Agreements*, 96.

54. Richard Rovere, "Tales Out of School," *New Yorker*, 16 March 1963, 195, cited in ibid.

55. Metzger, *Trade Agreements*, 96.

56. Ibid., 94–95.

57. Evans, *The Kennedy Round*, 299.

58. Ibid., 300.

59. Ibid., 301.

60. Ibid., 303.

61. Ibid., 310–311.

62. Ibid.

63. Ibid.

64. Ibid., 304.

65. Ibid., 304–305.

66. Ibid., 305.

67. Ibid., 305–306.

68. Ibid.

69. Ibid., 309.

70. Ibid., 303–304.

71. Nixon, *Public Papers of the Presidents of the United States* (Washington, D.C.: U.S. Government Printing Office, 1969).

72. Ibid.

73. Ibid., emphasis in original.

74. Ibid., 940–941.

75. Ibid., 941.

76. Ibid.

77. Ibid., 942.

78. Ibid.

79. Ibid.

80. Ibid.

81. Ibid., 943. The Trade Act was voted on in Congress in 1970, accounting for the disparity in dates.

82. Nixon, *Public Papers 1969*, 943.

83. Ibid.

84. Ibid., 944.

85. Ibid.

86. Ibid., 945.

87. Ibid., 945–946.

88. Allen Schick, *Making Economic Policy in Congress* (Washington, D.C.: American Enterprise Institute, 1983), 171.

89. Ibid., 175.

90. Nixon, *Public Papers 1971*, 886.

91. Ibid., 888–889, emphasis in original.

92. Ibid., emphasis in original.

93. Ibid.

94. Ibid., 889.

95. Ibid.

96. Ibid.

97. Ibid.

98. Ibid., 890.

99. Ibid.

100. Ibid.

101. Ibid.

102. Ibid.

103. Nixon, *Public Papers 1974*, 59–60.

104. Ibid.

105. Ibid., 60.

106. Ibid., 98.

107. Ibid., 624.

108. Ibid.

109. Schick, *Making Economic Policy*, 175–176.

110. Ibid., 176.

111. Mancur Olson, *The Rise and Decline of Nations* (New Haven: Yale University Press, 1982), 2.

112. Schick, *Making Economic Policy*, 160.

113. Ibid., 160–161.

114. Ibid.

115. Samuel Kemell, *Going Public: New Strategies of Presidential Leadership* (Washington, D.C.: Congressional Quarterly Press, 1986), 225.

116. Ryan C. Amacher, Gottfried Haberler, and Thomas D. Willett, *Challenges to a Liberal International Economic Order* (Washington, D.C.: American Enterprise Institute, 1979), 231.

117. Robert B. Reich, *The Next American Frontier* (New York: Penguin Books, 1984), 269.

118. Evans, *The Kennedy Round*, 29.

119. See ibid.

120. Ibid.

121. Robert B. Reich, *Tales of a New America* (New York: Random House, 1987), 83.

122. Reich, *Next American Frontier*, 323.

123. I. M. Destler, *American Trade Politics* (Washington, D.C.: Institute for International Economics and the Twentieth Century Fund, 1986), 45.

124. Ibid., 44–45.

125. Bauer, Pool, and Dexter, *American Business*, 19.

126. Ibid.

127. Judith L. Goldstein, "A Re-examination of American Trade Policy: An Inquiry in to the Causes of Protectionism" (Ph.D. dissertation, University of California, Los Angeles, 1983), 185.

128. Destler, *American Trade Politics*, 49.

129. Robert D. Hormats, "The Presidency in the High Competition, Hi-Tech Eighties," *Presidential Studies Quarterly*, 13 (Spring 1983): 258.

Chapter Three

President Reagan's Trade Rhetoric: Maintaining Consistency Despite Increasing Interdependence and a Growing Trade Deficit

America's economy underwent a major transformation in the 1980s as the United States for the first time became a debtor nation. While President Reagan's term in office was marked by a return of national optimism, the budget deficit and resultant trade deficit escalated to new heights during his administration, posing substantial problems for trade policy and, thus, trade rhetoric. The Reagan administration was the first presidential administration to confront heightened international economic competition. It balanced domestic pressures with foreign policy requirements by relying on the rhetoric of the free market despite engaging in market intervention. President Reagan's actions on trade shifted from successfully resisting protectionist pressures to proposing protectionist legislation, yet he managed to maintain a consistent rhetoric. Reagan was able to reconcile pragmatic policy shifts, in the form of limited protection and intervention in the market, with a conservative economic philosophy expressly forbidding market intervention.

President Reagan repeatedly relied on four rhetorical strategies in his approach to trade issues. First, he did not put these issues high on the public agenda, instead limiting himself to short radio addresses, talks to carefully selected audiences that experienced specific problems and would be affected by his policies, and speeches at economic summit meetings. This strategy had a three-fold purpose. It was intended to, first, avoid making trade a major public issue; second, to avoid elevating the criticism by his political opponents to the level of public consciousness; and third, achieve rhetorical consistency in the administration.

Reagan's second rhetorical strategy addressed the conflict between his words and actions. He based his support on his belief in the free market, but he conditioned his support for free trade on the practical reality of fair markets, grounded in his use of consistent themes rather than defenses of particular policies.

Reagan's third rhetorical strategy was to redefine free trade as fair trade in order to justify his administration's protectionist policies. He also insisted that such measures were only temporary and only defensive—policies adopted in response to unfair trade practices by other countries. This argument from redefinition allowed Reagan to take limited protectionist actions in the name of fair trade while remaining consistent with the principle of free trade.

Reagan's fourth rhetorical strategy was argument from polarization. His rhetoric on trade was built on the polar division of individual freedom versus government intervention. With domestic audiences, Reagan emphasized the more specific choice of free trade versus protectionism. With foreign audiences, he emphasized the overarching choice between individual freedom versus government intervention.

These four rhetorical strategies were consistently used by President Reagan in advocating and defending his trade policies. The latter three strategies—belief in the free market, redefining free trade as fair trade, and arguing from polarization—were not unique to the president. What was novel about these strategies was the consistency with which they were used—which was essential in the television age and the era of the modern rhetorical presidency. It is the first strategy, however, that most distinguishes the trade rhetoric of the Reagan presidency. Despite the passage of two major trade bills and the proposal of wide-ranging trade initiatives aimed at regionalization, Reagan made no prominent push for trade legislation. To a large measure, the extent of his success is directly attributable to his ability to keep trade off the public agenda. In this chapter, I examine each of these four strategies, with special attention devoted to how each strategy evolved over the course of the administration in response to changes in trade policy.

PRESIDENT REAGAN'S TRADE POLICY

Between 1981 and 1984 President Reagan maintained an overall policy of free trade, as consistent with his driving ideal of limited government. However, during this time public opinion and intensified congressional pressure impelled him to take select protectionist actions. The Reagan administration's direction in trade policy, after an initial period of confusion, emerged in 1981, when Reagan appointed William Brock as special trade representative. This appointment highlighted the relative weight of politics and economics in determining trade policy, as Brock was selected, not for his knowledge of trade (he had no special knowledge or experience), but rather for his "powers of compromise" and "conciliatory manner."[1] Brock himself admitted, "I have a lot to learn in the foreign trade area."[2] Consistent with past executives, the administration favored free trade but was willing to make exceptions to this overall policy as politically necessary.

In 1981, the administration allowed voluntary export restraints on automobiles from Japan but let expire quotas on shoes. Reagan's decision reflected political pragmatics: "The politics of automobiles are different from shoes. The President had campaigned in Michigan and other auto-producing states with the promise of curbs against the Japanese. He made no similar pledge in the shoe producing states."[3] Given this inconsistency, the administration united behind a white paper presenting a consistent rhetorical front in support of free trade, with an emphasis on the enforcement of free market rules. A July summit meeting of the industrialized countries provided an opportunity for the Reagan administration to continue its emphasis on free trade.

In 1982, protectionist pressures continued to escalate as the U.S. trade deficit reached a new high of $6.91 billion. Nonetheless, Reagan continued to publically defend free trade principles while following a policy of privately persuading other nations to open their markets to U.S. exports. Prior to the international economic summit in June, Japan's prime minister, Zenko Suzuki, called on the Japanese people to buy imports. The Reagan administration heralded Suzuki's appeal as a fundamental shift in Japanese's economic policy that went to the root of the problem—Japan's reluctance to import. The economic summit itself produced another united call for free trade yet achieved little in actual deficit reduction or the opening of markets. Thus protectionist pressures continued, fueled by midterm elections. The Reagan administration tried to contain damages with a Congress more susceptible to protectionist pressures by announcing three actions designed to alleviate the deficit and, thus, public concern: limiting steel imports, extending voluntary export restraints on autos, and funding the promotion of exports. The administration renewed its support for the principle of free trade at the November meeting of the General Agreement on Tariffs and Trade (GATT). The administration had called this international meeting, without public fanfare, for the express purpose of restricting both tariff and nontariff barriers. GATT involves a long and arduous process. As in the 1981 economic summit, the international leaders agreed to a statement supporting the principle of free trade. More important, however, the GATT meeting provided the impetus for further negotiations to eliminate trade barriers.

By 1983, the continued high trade deficit had heightened an internal struggle within the Reagan administration over the relationship of the strong dollar and the trade deficit. At the May economic summit, held in Williamsburg, Virginia, leaders of the industrialized countries denounced the U.S. budget deficit. At the September meeting of the IMF and the World Bank, international leaders again attacked America's budget deficit. Although administration officials began to leak intentions to devalue the dollar, President Reagan continued to defend the strong dollar as a sign of a strong economy. Economically, this argument was sound, but politically, as the high trade deficit continued, Reagan's defense of the strong dollar was costly. To counter the political costs of maintaining a strong dollar, the administration continued to fight for reciprocity.

Nineteen eighty-four was an election year. Trade resurfaced as a weapon for the Democrats to use to attack Reagan and the Republican members of Congress. The administration continued to follow an overall policy of free trade but stressed fairness—the principle of reciprocity—and therefore advocated the elimination of restrictions on trade by foreign nations. Reagan emphasized that America could compete if given a "level playing field." The administration thus based its support for free trade in faith in America's competitiveness, in the executive tradition, and more important in with the campaign theme, "America is back and standing tall." The annual economic summit (G–7 Summit of the Industrialized Nations including the United States, France, Germany, Japan, U.K., Canada, and Italy) in June 1984 in London provided Reagan with an opportunity to publicly protect American trading interests abroad through pushing for fair trade. On the domestic front, the administration compromised with Congress in producing the Trade and Tariff Act of 1984. The administration agreed to cut steel imports through voluntary restraints, and Congress in turn eliminated protectionist amendments. There was no major public push for passage, for to do so would only aggravate protectionist pressures, highlight administration compromises, and strengthen Congress's hand.

In September 1985, the Reagan administration devalued the dollar—which was a fundamental policy shift. Admittedly, the administration had taken limited protectionist actions in its first four years, most publicly in autos and steel. However, the devaluation of the dollar was Reagan's first flagrant violation of the functioning of the marketplace. Intervention had finally emerged from the depths of the administration infighting—which previously had undermined any cohesive trade policy. Protectionist pressure at a crisis level, preventing the administration from focusing on its priorities of tax reform and a United States–Soviet summit, had forced a policy change:

> Until recently, such thinking was heresy within the Reagan camp. Administration monetarists, led by Secretary of State George P. Shultz and Council of Economic Advisers Chairman Beryl W. Sprinkel, argued that the value of the dollar was set by market forces and that over- or under-valuation was impossible by definition. When he was at Treasury, White House Chief of Staff Donald T. Regan generally agreed. But [Treasury Secretary, James] Baker and [Deputy Chief of Staff to Baker, Richard] Darman are pragmatists who see nothing wrong with a little tinkering to improve the international monetary system. "You can't address the trade problem without looking at the dollar," says Darman. Egged on by the Treasury Duo, President Reagan—who has repeatedly cited the dollar's strength as a sign of America's economic muscle—agreed to the policy switch.[4]

Devaluation of the dollar was akin to Nixon's divorce of the dollar from the gold standard with market intervention—a remarkable broach of free trade theory. Successfully keeping trade off the public agenda, even in this case of critical intervention, explains Reagan's ability to maintain a consistent rhetoric adhering to limited government involvement in the free market. The Reagan administration continued its policy of pushing for free but fair trade through 1986, 1987, and 1988, employing select protectionist actions and the continued devaluation of the dollar.

The Reagan administration did not actively seek trade legislation in 1986 but pursued its export-led trade policy through three proceedings: bilateral talks with Canada, an international economic summit in Tokyo, and a call for GATT negotiations. Meanwhile, proposed trade legislation continued to pass through the House and Senate, although the Reagan administration managed to sustain a veto of legislation proposing textile quotas. In the 1986 midterm elections, Reagan put his prestige on the line in campaigning for Senate Republicans, which caused Democrats to view trade as a liability for the administration and for Republicans in Congress. Thus Reagan was dealt a severe political blow as the Democrats regained control of the Senate. With a Democratically controlled House and Senate, the administration moved toward a trade policy of compromise. To demonstrate its commitment to fair trade, the administration imposed duties against EEC agricultural imports on 30 December 1986.

In 1987 and 1988, the administration and Congress could agree on one trade theme—the need for competitiveness. Dennis Whitfield, deputy secretary of labor, stated: "No matter whether you're Democrat or Republican, liberal or conservative, everyone's for a more competitive economy."[5] The administration had two goals with this theme of competitiveness: first, to decrease the likelihood of protectionist legislation; and second, to deflect attention from the Iran-contra scandal.

To enhance its chances for success in trade negotiations with Congress, the administration imposed a tariff on electronic imports from Japan. The administration's drive for fair trade at the 1987 Venice economic summit (G–7 Summit of Industrialized Nations) was eclipsed by the political controversy over U.S. escorting of Kuwaiti tankers through the Persian Gulf. In spite of the administration tariffs on Japan and international economic negotiations, protectionist trade legislation passed the House and the Senate. Congressional pressure for protectionism was further heightened when the Toshiba scandal broke. In 1987, the sale of sensitive technology to the Soviet Union by a Toshiba Corporation subsidiary, in violation of Japanese law and international agreements, resulted in increased pressure for protectionist legislation directed against Japan. Japanese Prime Minister Yasuhiro Nakasone's visit to the United States to address the United Nations did little to douse the protectionist flames.

Despite these primarily negative events in trade, the administration did achieve one success in the name of free trade: the United States–Canada bilateral trade pact. In addition, the 1988 Omnibus Trade and Competitiveness Act was not as protectionist as originally feared by the administration. While it did require retaliation if countries maintained a persistent trade imbalance, this clause actually allowed the administration to take trade-restricting actions in the name of fair trade while placing responsibility for those actions on Congress. The administration could say it was acting in the name of fair trade, having been forced because other nations had violated free trade rules. The administration could therefore say it remained committed to the principle of free trade. This was a rhetorical reality, and thus a political bill, that Reagan could accept.

From 1981 through 1988, the Reagan administration's trade policy thus encompassed limited protectionist actions, two major trade bills, and intervention in the market. Despite these dramatic changes in policy, the Reagan administration managed to keep trade off the public agenda, defend free trade, promote fair trade, and contrast the benefits of the free market with the perils of government intervention.

KEEPING TRADE OFF THE PUBLIC AGENDA

Presidents traditionally have found it to their advantage to keep trade off the public agenda. Making trade an issue activates the inherently protectionist public, which is disadvantageous for the free trade–oriented executive. However, keeping trade off the public agenda does not translate into ignoring the persuasive possibilities of television—especially the network news. The Reagan administration capitalized on the new persuasive possibilities open to the president, seizing on Reagan's ability to be seen by the public through the mass media as an activist leader. In trade, this translated into visuals of Reagan protecting American interests abroad at international economic meetings. Indeed, given the general conclusions of international economic proclamations, these photo opportunities were the most outstanding benefit of international economic summits. The visual impact was also the primary determinant in selecting the audiences for Reagan's trade speeches: examples include Reagan's 1984 speech at a Ford Motor factory and his 1987 speech at a Harley-Davidson plant. An administration aide admitted the partisan motives behind the Kansas City Ford factory visit: "While the trip was described as a nonpolitical one financed by the taxpayers, Reagan aides privately conceded the visit was designed largely to produce television news pictures closely identifying an ebullient-looking President with booming industrial settings."[6] Thus, even though Reagan was wandering into hostile territory—into a factory where consolidation had actually cost jobs and where the union had endorsed Walter Mondale, not Reagan—it was the pictures, not the actual speech, that was most important to the Reagan team. The visuals were important for the administration to show the president acting to promote free trade abroad and protect fair trade at home.

However, the Reagan administration did not exploit the ability of the president to command a national audience through televised speeches on trade. To focus attention on trade as an issue through a major televised speech would be to highlight the administration's failure in resolving the trade deficit, as well as Reagan's capitulations to protectionist pressures. Herein was the major challenge for Reagan's rhetoric on trade. Reagan needed to satisfy foreign nations that he was truly trying to preserve free trade through open markets while convincing domestic actors that he was pushing for fair trade and would act to protect American interests if necessary.

Thus, in his first term, President Reagan attempted to resolve the trade deficit on a piecemeal basis through limited protectionist actions. To reconcile these actions with free market principles, Reagan chose to minimize these actions through select, limited announcements to the affected audiences. The only public strategy was Reagan's presence at international economic summits, where the administration presented him as fighting to open markets to protect American interests abroad. This strategy was ineffective, however. Without a coordinated and public offensive to diminish the trade deficit, the Reagan administration seemed to Congress to be ignoring a very real problem. As the trade deficit worsened, the public image of an ineffective administration increased in potency. The administration's decision to privately address foreign nations' violation of marketplace rules contributed to the image of an administration unwilling to defend America's trading interests. Trade was an especially volatile issue during the election years:

The intensity of the trade debate can be explained by that one word: jobs. The issue first came into focus last month, when the Democrats managed to hold on, narrowly, to a Texas Congressional seat by stressing the impact of foreign trade on local employment. "When trade turned out to be a cutting issue, when it brought people back to the Democratic banner, everyone was off to the races," said Representative Thomas F. Petri, a Wisconsin Republican. As they traveled their home districts during last month's recess many lawmakers from both parties have said, they were overwhelmed by the expression of voter resentment against the loss of jobs to foreign competition.[7]

However, public opinion favoring tariffs had actually declined. A Gallup poll found that while 78 percent of the American public rated "protecting the jobs of American workers" as a principal goal of American foreign policy, only 53 percent believed tariffs were necessary (down from 57 percent in 1978). Moreover, 28 percent favored eliminating tariffs (up from 22 percent).[8] This contradiction in public opinion between widespread support for protection of American jobs and lesser support for specific actions to protect these jobs reflected the complex and cross-cutting nature of trade policy:

Most analysts see the public's perception of trade issues as confused and ambivalent. That is because trade cuts across jobs and the cost of living in conflicting ways.

Polls show that when people think their economic security is threatened by imports, they react in a protectionist fashion. On the other hand, when they are reminded that protectionism means higher prices and limits on their choice of consumer goods, they come down more for free trade.[9]

Thus there exists a conundrum in trade policy. The executive, as foreign policy leader, has consistently favored free trade. The legislative branch, representing various constituencies, has consistently favored protectionism (in the postwar years, as reflective of public opinion). However, the executive is also beholden to domestic constituencies. The president must balance foreign policy considerations with domestic economic interests. While this particular problem has been consistent throughout U.S. history, economic conditions since the 1980s have elevated this political and rhetorical problem to its greatest heights. The pervasiveness of the media (the growing importance of television, especially) as a check to presidential power, has heightened the president's dilemma of reconciling foreign and domestic interests in trade.[10]

FREE TRADE AND FREE MARKETS

President Reagan's push for open markets and general condemnation of tariffs on U.S. imports began to be perceived by the public as an inadequate defense of American interests. The president's rhetorical task seemed difficult, if not impossible. His conservative economic philosophy did not allow for government intervention in the market. In fact, Reagan supported two aims for government: providing for the national defense and for the truly needy. His support for a free market further mitigated against intrusion in the economy. To publicly break with his economic belief in the free market would seriously undermine Reagan's governing philosophy. However, the president was also a pragmatic politician. He was politically successful in part because he was willing to bend his political philosophies as necessitated by the circumstances. Therefore, one key to his governing success was his very ability to reconcile these pragmatic policy shifts with his consistent governing principles. Reagan's rhetorical skill thus, in large part, accounted for his political success.

At the core of Reagan's trade rhetoric was his ideological commitment to free trade based on free markets. Reagan defended the principle of free trade ardently because it was grounded in the very ideals of a democracy. Even after intervening in the market by devaluing the dollar, in September 1985, Reagan remained adamant about this basic principle:

And let me say at the outset that our trade policy rests firmly on the foundation of free trade and open markets, free trade. I, like you, recognize the inescapable conclusion that all of history has taught, the freer the flow of world trade, the stronger the tides for human progress and peace among nations. I certainly don't have to explain the benefits of free and open markets to you. They produce more jobs, a more productive standard of living. They strengthen our national security because our economy, the bedrock of our defense, is stronger.[11]

Reagan further minimized this philosophical break in his actions with a deliberately vague description of devaluation: "But yesterday I authorized Treasury Secretary Baker to join his counterparts from other major industrial countries to announce measures to promote stronger and more balanced growth in our economies and thereby the strengthening of foreign currencies."[12] He remained on the offensive, emphasizing growth. True to the executive tradition, the administration stressed productivity—the belief in Americans' ability to compete:

In speeches and in informal meetings, Mr. Brock has been delivering a simple message: The way to compete with foreign business is to compete. "We have got to combat the idea of American trade inferiority by demonstrating our strengths," he says. "Words are not going to do it. We have to do it by competing."

Increasing the nation's competitiveness has emerged as one of the major themes of Mr. Brock's tenure as trade representative. He has, for example, told America industrial leaders: "It's not the business of Government to protect against failure." On another occasion, he urged American companies to "get off our duff and start competing."[13]

The administration attempted to sell their decision to focus on the promotion of exports as belief in the very ability of Americans to produce. The Reagan administration was challenging America to believe in itself. Reagan's optimistic rhetoric reinforced this policy. Indeed, he premised his support for free trade on his belief in the American people. Speaking at a Pennsylvania Harley-Davidson plant in 1987, Reagan stated:

Some people said that you couldn't make the grade. They said you couldn't keep up with foreign competition. They said that Harley-Davidson was running out of gas and sputtering to a stop. Well, the people who say that American workers and American companies can't compete are making one of the oldest mistakes in the world. They're betting against America itself, and that's one bet no one will ever win. Like America, Harley is back and standing tall.[14]

In his rhetoric, Reagan emphasized that protectionist policies were self-defeating. The trade imbalance would improve as world economies grew, assuming adherence to free trade principles. The administration continued to enlarge the scope of the debate, emphasizing export-led growth: "What needs to be done, President Reagan told a group of business people at the White House, is to 'shift the political focus away from negative, protectionist legislation to positive pro-growth policies—policies like comprehensive tax reform and spending reductions.' "[15] Therefore, in 1986 the administration began a new offensive based on "competitiveness," a term that was adopted by both Democrats and Republicans. As one trade lawyer commented: "To the trade professionals, competitiveness is a buzzword. . . . For the Democrats, it's a way to say, 'We're not protectionists,' as they write their protectionist legislation. For the Republicans, it's a way to say, 'We are not single-minded free traders.' "[16] The theme of competitiveness enhanced the administration's definition of free trade as fair trade; of growth through exports via free markets versus declinism through protection via closed markets.

FREE TRADE DEFINED AS FAIR TRADE

To promote free trade, President Reagan needed to defeat protection. To do this, reciprocity came to the forefront of administration rhetoric, as Reagan defined free trade as fair trade:

The United States will reject protectionist and defeatist proposals. Instead, we will set new goals and lay out a program for limiting government intervention in world markets. We will lead with a clear sense of our own commercial interests and a quiet determination to defend these interests. We will take actions at home and abroad which will enhance the ability of United States industries to compete in international trade.

Let no one misunderstand us. We're generous and farsighted in our goals, and we intend to use our full power to achieve these goals. We seek to plug the holes in the boat of free markets and free trade and get it moving again in the direction of prosperity. And no one should mistake our determination to use our full power and influence to prevent others from destroying the boat and sinking us all.[17]

For Reagan, the mandate for defeating protection was grounded in the lessons of history, with the Smoot-Hawley Act a potent rhetorical symbol: "For those of us who lived through the Great Depression, the memory of the suffering it caused is deep and searing. And today many economic analysts and historians argue that high tariff legislation passed back in that period called the Smoot-Hawley tariff greatly deepened the depression and prevented economic recovery."[18]

As had Nixon, President Reagan used the power of his office to educate, defining protection as economically disastrous despite its apparent short-term benefits:

You see, at first, when someone says, "Let's impose tariffs on foreign imports," it looks like they're doing the patriotic thing by protecting American products and jobs. And sometimes for a short while it works—but only for a short time. What eventually occurs is: First, homegrown industries start relying on government protection in the form of high tariffs. They stop competing and stop making innovative management and technological changes they need to succeed in world markets. And then, while all this is going on, something even worse occurs. High tariffs inevitably lead to retaliation by foreign countries and the triggering of fierce trade wars. The result is more and more tariffs, higher and higher trade barriers, and less and less competition. So, soon, because of the prices made artificially high by tariffs that subsidize inefficiency and poor management, people stop buying. Then the worst happens: Markets shrink and collapse; businesses and industries shut down; and millions of people lose their jobs.[19]

Reagan explicitly rejected formal quotas. The president continued his pedantic tone in explaining his August 1985 decision not to impose quotas on shoes, saying: "Quotas would have entitled our trading partners to another $2 billion in compensations or they would have retaliated, slapping quotas or tariffs on the products we sell to them. That would mean an immediate loss of American jobs and a dangerous step down the road to a trade war. Also, if our trading partners can't sell their products here, they can't afford to buy our exports and that means more lost jobs for Americans."[20]

However, the Reagan administration did impose market-restricting tariffs. Reagan reconciled free trade policy with trade-restricting measures under the rubric of fair trade. In explaining his decision to impose tariffs on Japanese semiconductors in April 1987, Reagan stated: "We had clear evidence that Japanese companies were engaging in unfair trade practices that violated an agreement between Japan and the United States. We expect our trading partners to live up to their agreements. As I've often said: Our commitment to free trade is also a commitment to fair trade."[21] Reagan emphasized that his administration was taking actions to ensure fair trade. Carrying through with the metaphor of the level playing field and the rules of competition, the president cited instances of aggressive, offensive action:

Now this doesn't absolve other nations from playing by the rules. Free trade means, by definition, fair trade. And where other nations aren't playing by the rules, this administration is more activist, more aggressive, than any other in blowing the whistle on unfair trade practices against American producers. In the past year alone we have gone after Korean abuse of intellectual property rights and we've increased access of American agricultural products to European and Taiwanese markets. And while we prefer to negotiate, we have taken and will take strong action when necessary against markets closed to American goods and services. And to prevent other countries from selling below cost and unfairly moving in on American markets, we have initiated 528 antidumping and countervailing duty cases.[22]

As protectionist pressures increased and the administration began to consider devaluing the dollar, fair trade rhetoric came to the forefront. In 1985, immediately prior to devaluation, the administration admitted that it was preparing a new trade strategy in hopes of satisfying Congress: " 'You have to emphasize not just the free trade of a free and open trading system but the fair-trade part,' a senior administration official said today. The aide provided details of what he described as a subtle but carefully calculated policy shift to align Mr. Reagan's position with the tougher mood in Congress and in the public."[23] As one lobbyist put it: "Free trade rhetoric is a loser politically, fair trade rhetoric is a winner."[24] Following devaluation, Reagan attributed the action, not to domestic economic failures, but rather to foreign nations' illicit practices: "I will not stand by and watch American businesses fail because of unfair trade practices abroad. I will not stand by and watch American workers lose their jobs because other nations do not play by the rules."[25] Because Reagan defined problems in trade as caused by other nations' failure to observe the rules of free trade, he was able to preserve his argument that his free market economic policies remained successful: "We have put incentives into our own economy to make it grow and create jobs. And, as you know, business has prospered. We have created over eight million new jobs in the last 33 months. Just since 1980, manufacturing production has increased 17 percent."[26]

In this speech announcing devaluation, Reagan closed by reaffirming his commitment to free markets and his administration's active role in defending American interests as well as ensuring American international economic leadership: "Our commitment to free trade is undiminished. We will vigorously pursue our policy of promoting free and open markets in this country and around the world. We will insist that all nations face up to their responsibilities of preserving and enhancing free trade everywhere."[27]

For the remainder of his term, President Reagan emphasized that free trade meant fair trade:

Well, let me restate, then, the trade policy of this administration. We will root out and take action against unfair trade practices targeted at American products or American workers. We will be alert and aggressive in opening up foreign markets closed to American exporters. We will bring the world with us into a new era of free and fair trade. Free trade with free traders is our byword.[28]

Stressing the fair in free and fair trade allowed Reagan to contrast his free market-based policy with his protectionist opponents. And this dualism was at the core of Reagan's economic rhetoric.

ARGUMENT FROM POLARIZATION

Reagan's conservative philosophy, his belief in limited government, remained the foundation of his trade rhetoric. Reagan's clear worldview and mindset of a moral United States versus a godless communist empire, provided the impetus for his polarized rhetoric.[29] Reagan's rhetoric on trade was built on the polar division of individual freedom versus government intervention. With domestic audiences, Reagan emphasized the more specific choice of free trade versus protection. With foreign audiences, Reagan emphasized the overarching principle of individual freedom versus government intervention. In adapting these fundamental polar divisions to suit situations and audiences, Reagan revealed in his rhetoric a hierarchy of arguments.

In speaking to domestic audiences, Reagan contrasted his role as president, protector of the national interest, with Congress, which he described as beholden to special interests:

I came to Washington to spare the American people the protectionist legislation that destroys prosperity. Now, it hasn't always been easy. There are those in this Congress, just as there were back in the thirties, who want to go for the quick political advantage, who will risk America's prosperity for the sake of a short-term appeal to some special interest group, who forget that more than 5 million American jobs are directly tied to the foreign export business and additional millions are tied to imports.[30]

True to the tradition of the executive, President Reagan emphasized export-led growth. He also ignored the persuasive possibilities open to a president pressured by congress in trade negotiations with foreign nations, instead attacking Congress as endangering the public via narrow special interests:

So, with my meeting with Prime Minister Nakasone and the Venice Economic Summit coming up, it's terribly important not to restrict a President's options in such trade dealings with foreign governments. Unfortunately, some in Congress are trying to do exactly that. I'll keep you informed on this dangerous legislation, because it's just another form of protectionism and I may need your help to stop it. Remember, America's jobs and growth are at stake.[31]

In speaking on the campaign trail, in addition to reliance on his role as protector of the national interest, Reagan contrasted the gloomy past with the brightness of the present and thus the hope for the future:

All of these are real solutions to the real problem of getting the world economy back on the growth track. And that's the track to a future of open vistas and unfolding opportunities, a future where we all grow together, where every nation's prosperity augments our own.

Unfortunately the House of Representatives last week turned its back on the future and started marching right back to Smoot-Hawley. Its so-called omnibus trade bill is really an ominous antitrade bill that could send our economy into the steepest nose-dive since the Great Depression. This reactionary legislation would force American consumers to pay billions in higher prices, throw millions of Americans out of work, and strangle our economy as foreign markets slam shut in retaliation.[32]

Reagan's optimism versus his opponents' pessimism was integral to this division. Moreover, Reagan contrasted his knowledge with his opponents' ignorance, his moral policy based on principle versus his opponents' preference for the merely expedient, and the permanence of his true solution—the free market—versus the temporary quick fix of protection. In his rhetoric, Reagan argued that his was a position of strength, while opponents' positions followed from a tradition of weakness: "We do not seek an America that is closed to the world; we seek a world that is open to America. We do not dream of protecting America from others' success; we seek to include everyone in the success of the American dream."[33]

In speaking to domestic audiences, all these themes—protecting the national interest and promoting an economically and politically strong present and future United States based on the free market—emphasized the wisdom and success of Reagan's policies, the past failures of Democratic administrations, and the weakness of Democratic alternatives. When attacking previous Democratic administrations, Reagan was attacking their domestic economic policies. He did not acknowledge previous presidents' adherence to the principle of free trade and, for the most part, allegiance to the practice of free trade. In particular, he did not acknowledge Republican president Hoover's contribution to the Smoot-Hawley Act or Hoover's support for the flexible tariff.

In speaking to foreign audiences, Reagan relied on the fundamental division of individual freedom versus government intervention. Inherent in this division was the contrast between the United States and the Soviet Union, representing the democratic versus the totalitarian system: "Millions of individuals making their own decisions in the marketplace will always allocate resources better than any centralized government planning process."[34] Nations could follow the U.S. example of the free market or enact controls, thus taking one step down the road toward economic restrictions.

Reagan's most frequently used trade metaphor was premised on these very polarizations:

We're in the same boat with our trading partners. If one partner shoots a hole in the boat, does it make sense for the other one to shoot another hole in the boat? Some say, yes, and call that getting tough. Well, I call it stupid. We shouldn't be shooting holes; we should be working together to plug them up. We must strengthen the boat of freer markets and fair trade so it can lead the world to economic recovery and greater political stability.[35]

This metaphor reinforced several of the polar divisions within Reagan's trade rhetoric: a sense of movement forward, or optimism, versus movement backward, or pessimism; and presidential wisdom and U.S. leadership versus congressional ignorance and partisan infighting. In Reagan's rhetoric, economic controls inevitably led to political controls: "Trust the people—this is the crucial lesson of history. Because only when the human spirit is allowed to worship, invent, create, and produce, only when individuals are given a personal stake in deciding their destiny and benefiting from their own risks, only then do societies become dynamic, prosperous, and free."[36] In Reagan's rhetoric, the United States was an active force responsible for leading the passive world, which Reagan portrayed as a victim. The United States was accorded this role of leader, not only because of divine providence, although this rationale was a part of Reagan's rhetoric, but also because of U.S. prosperity. Reagan connected U.S. economic prosperity with political stability and security. At the core of the nation's economic strength was the principle of the free market: "We will not seek false security behind restrictive quotas and import duties. Nations that hide behind tariff walls soon fall behind. America's destiny is not to be second or third or fourth in the march to the future. It's to be in the vanguard, leading the free nations into a brighter and better era."[37] The dualisms in Reagan's rhetoric were consistent: protectionism would result in the failures of the past; free trade would lead to a successful future.

Reagan's presidential rhetoric was consistent in its worldview and moral stance. He divided the world into two halves: good and evil; communist and noncommunist. Reagan's continuous casting of the United States versus the Soviet Union exemplified Philip Wander's concept of prophetic dualism. In addition, the elaboration of this theme—as Wander writes, the "religious cast to public discourse"—was evident in Reagan's rhetoric.[38] Reagan's dualisms often pitted nations against each other: most notably, the free market versus government intervention in the form of the United States versus the Soviet Union.

With the easing, and now end, of the Cold War, a new opposition has arisen, that of the United States versus Japan. Economic competition has replaced military competition, which Wander labels "technocratic realism."[39] Therein lay the danger in the Reagan administration's policy in promoting exports and exhorting the American worker to compete. Boosting American pride through competitiveness inflamed nationalistic passions, especially in reelection years when the search for a scapegoat reached its heights. For example, in the midst of the 1982 recession, Representative John D. Dingell, Democrat of Michigan, attacked the "little yellow people" as responsible for competition that had damaged the American auto industry.[40] Representative Lyle Williams, a moderate Republican from the auto- and steel-producing Mahoning Valley in Ohio, called for "economic war" against Japan: "The enemy in this country, and it's a damaging enemy, is imports."[41] Representative James A. Courter, Republican from New Jersey, viewed these calls for protection as scapegoating: "People like to blame their problems on events beyond their control. They don't like to look within themselves."[42]

In addition to the ease of uniting against an outsider, Democrats found it easier to attack the Japanese than to attack Reagan: "Because many Democrats are still wary attacking President Reagan head-on, protectionist rhetoric is becoming more common on the campaign trail. 'You've got a lot of Democrats who are afraid to blame Reaganomics for the country's economic woes,' says a Senate Democratic aide, 'so they blame the Japanese instead.' "[43] Increased congressional pressure for protection was an election year ritual: "Free trade, history has shown, is a doctrine of prosperity, expendable in a time of hardship, particularly when elections loom. 'A lot of these Congressmen have problems in their districts and they need someone to blame,' says Frank A. Well, a Washington attorney who was Deputy Secretary of Commerce during the Carter administration. 'Japan is that someone. I think it's only realistic to expect some kind of legislation this year.' "[44]

Democratic presidential candidate Walter Mondale campaigned in favor of domestic content, announcing: "We've been running up the white flag. What do we want our kids to do? Sweep up around Japanese computers?"[45] However, in President Reagan's trade rhetoric, Japan did not replace the Soviet Union as the enemy. While Reagan acknowledged that trade barriers between countries existed, he attacked the barriers, not the particular country: "Our trading partners must join us in working to improve the system of trade that has contributed so much to economic growth and the security of our allies and ourselves."[46] Reagan had to balance his role as leader of the nation in the international arena with domestic policy concerns. During Reagan's term of office, security concerns still outweighed economic constraints.

CONCLUSION

Reagan's presidency trade policy evolved into a significant issue due to both increased public attention and fundamental economic changes. The Reagan administration was consistent it its rhetoric despite revolutionary policy changes. First, the administration did not put trade issues high on the public agenda. Reagan made no televised speech devoted solely to the trade issue, in contrast with major speeches on other economic problems, such as inflation, unemployment, and taxes. When he proposed policies to deal with the other economic problems, he used television to gain the widest possible audience and greatest possible support. With trade issues, however, he limited himself to short radio addresses, talks to carefully selected audiences that experienced specific problems and would be affected by his policies, and speeches at economic summit meetings.

This strategy had a three-fold purpose. It was intended to avoid making trade a major public issue. By not speaking on national television with a speech devoted solely to the trade issue, the president avoided making it a public priority of his administration. Public attention to trade would result in an increase in public awareness, and consequently, the activation of the portion of the public most likely to favor protectionism. Rather, one key to Reagan's rhetorical success on trade was his ability to reach the affected publics with his limited protectionist actions: to reassure them that he was indeed taking action and not ignoring the trade imbalance. Moreover, this strategy was intended to avoid elevating the criticism by his political opponents to the level of public consciousness. Instead, he treated it, for the most part, as just another issue to be managed, rather than a "crisis" to be addressed. This diminished the effectiveness of opponents' arguments by seeming to fail to respond directly. Finally, President Reagan sought rhetorical consistency in his administration. However, his policies of selective protection for some industries—even on a temporary basis—seemed to contradict his well-known belief in free trade. Speaking often and on high-visibility platforms about his policies would give the media and his opponents the opportunity to highlight the difference between his words and actions. Therefore, the president kept his rhetoric low-key by using only radio addresses and appropriate occasions (such as summit meetings) to speak on the issue.

However, when Reagan did speak, he had to address the conflict between his words and actions, and this led to his second strategy. To resolve this conflict, he did what previous presidents had done: he based his support for free trade on his belief in the free market. However, Reagan conditioned his support for free trade on the practical reality of fair markets. Previous presidents have conditioned support for free trade on the principle of reciprocity. They made exceptions to the principle of free trade—some more than others—even as they held up free trade as the economic ideal. The strategy the administration used was grounded in Reagan's use of consistent themes rather than defenses of particular policies. The president consistently upheld the ideal of free trade as the theme and goal of his administration. During his second term in office, Reagan added the themes of strength and competitiveness. Each of his policies, he asserted, was intended to create free trade by drawing on the strength of American industry and workers and increasing the competitiveness of the American economy. Regardless of which policy he was advocating or defending, Reagan placed it within the themes of free trade, strength, and competitiveness. Thus, policies that might have been interpreted as inconsistent were made consistent by shifting their rhetorical basis from specific policies to the themes that the president persistently voiced.

However, this strategy of thematic consistency would not have been effective had the administration not used a corollary strategy to account for particular changes in policy. When he had to initiate protectionist policies, such as devaluing the dollar or protecting individual industries, Reagan redefined free trade as fair trade to justify those measures. However, he also insisted that such measures were only temporary and only defensive—policies adopted in response to unfair practices by other countries. This argument from redefinition allowed Reagan to take limited protectionist actions in the name of fair trade while remaining consistent with the principles of free trade, competitiveness, and maintaining America's economic strength. In essence, as had previous Presidents, Reagan redefined free trade as fair trade. Thus, he circumvented conflicts among his administration policies by arguing that actions on behalf of fair trade were necessary to preserve free trade. He would announce with regret that the administration had been forced by the unfair trading practices of other nations to take restrictive actions to preserve free trade. Reagan never labeled his actions as "protectionist" but rather termed them actions intended to restore a balance that would lead to his goal of freer trade. According to Reagan, other nations violated the rules of free trade, and thus the United States had to respond by enforcing the rules through temporary fair trade restrictions, which would eventually be lifted when balance was restored and free trade allowed to flourish.

When Reagan recognized the political severity of the trade deficit in 1985 and devalued the dollar, his rhetorical strategies stood their severest test. The president had to reconcile devaluation with his previous defense of the strong dollar, and furthermore, he had to reconcile intervention in the international market with his repeated opposition to government intervention in the economic markets. To meet these contradictions, Reagan denied that devaluation was intervention in the international market. To soften the impact of devaluation, the Reagan administration preceded devaluation with hints from administration officials that the strong dollar might indeed be a cause of the trade deficit. Reagan himself did not publicly retract his claims of success for the strong dollar, which he had repeatedly made during the first four years. Instead, after devaluation, Reagan began to emphasize the "fair" aspect of free and fair trade even more strongly and to trumpet his administration's actions in specific unfair trading cases, the strong dollar being the most prominent in this move from a defensive to an offensive stance. President Reagan's rhetoric was successful insofar as he was able to redefine political compromises as consistent with principle.

The fourth and final strategy Reagan used was argument from polarization. Reagan's rhetoric on trade was built on the polar division of individual freedom versus government intervention. With domestic audiences, the president emphasized the more specific choice of free trade versus protectionism. With foreign audiences, he emphasized the overarching choice between individual freedom versus government intervention.

Reagan did not merely ground his support for free trade in fair trade. He did not just rely on abstract economic arguments or redefining particular issues. To have done so would have been to share the argumentative ground with Democrats, who also premised their trade policies on the ideal of the free market. Instead, Reagan explicitly contrasted his trade policies with his opponents' alternatives and argued that he was acting in the national interest while his congressional opponents were acting from narrow partisan concerns. He contrasted his policy based on principle with his opponents' preferences for policies based on expediency. Thus, he made the choice a choice between a permanent solution—letting the free market function fully—and a temporary "quick fix"—immediate protectionist measures. Reagan argued that his position was one of strength because it was enduring, whereas his opponents had succumbed to panicky solutions that betrayed weakness. In making these polarizing arguments, Reagan concluded that his policies would unleash the great economic forces in America and lead to prosperity, whereas Democratic policies would repeat the mistakes of Smoot-Hawley and lead to another Depression.

In speaking to foreign audiences, Reagan relied on the fundamental division between individual freedom and government intervention. Inherent in this division was a contrast between the United States and the Soviet Union, or the democratic and totalitarian systems. Nations had a choice: they could follow the example of the United States and follow the path of the free market, which led to political freedom. Alternately, they could enact restrictions and take the path to government control and a loss of political freedom. In his rhetoric, Reagan argued that economic controls inevitably led to political controls.

Even though Reagan's rhetorical strategies were successful to the degree that they reconciled fundamental policy shifts with his belief in the free market, they failed to take into account the economic realities of interdependence. Most important, Reagan's economic beliefs disallowed intervention in the economy. Thus, when intervention was necessary to fight for fair trade, he had to minimize the actions. Presidents who must disown their actual intervention in the economy diminish their ability to manage economic transformations and to minimize the political costs of economic dislocation by overtly providing economic alternatives. While Reagan demonstrated that intervention could be reconciled with a free trade rhetoric, his disavowal of protectionist actions eliminated the potential of an escape valve for protectionist pressure. President Reagan's ability to control the public agenda, in this instance on trade, serves as a powerful rhetorical model for future presidents. His ability to govern according to consistent themes, in this case reconciling protectionist actions with a free trade rhetoric, also serves as a fount of rhetorical power for future executives. Nonetheless, both principles—controlling the agenda and governing according to consistent themes—must be used for different purposes in trade rhetoric. Government intervention may be necessary to preserve free trade in an interdependent economy that is increasingly subject to dislocations of labor and the persistent use of nontariff barriers. Moreover, in the post–Cold War world, the increasing importance of economic competition merely heightens the pressures on the executive. In the following years, Presidents George Bush and Bill Clinton were subject to these heightened cross-pressures as they had to balance international trade negotiations—embodied by NAFTA and GATT—with a continued high trade deficit further inflating protectionist pressures.

NOTES

A version of this chapter originally appeared as Delia B. Conti, "President Reagan's Trade Rhetoric: Lessons for the 1990's," *Presidential Studies Quarterly*, no. 1, 25:1 (Winter 1995): 91–108. Permission granted by the Center for the Study of the Presidency, publisher of *Presidential Studies Quarterly*.

1. Howell Raines, "Brock Appointed by Reagan to Be Trade Representative," *New York Times*, 16 January 1981, 2:5.

2. Ibid.

3. Clyde H. Farnsworth, "Free Trade and Politics: New Tests for Reagan," *New York Times*, 5 July 1981, 1:26.

4. Lee Walczak et al., "The New Trade Strategy," *Business Week*, 7 October 1985, 94.

5. Kenneth B. Noble, "The Clamor for 'Competitiveness,' " *New York Times*, 12 January 1987, 1:14.

6. Francis X. Clines, "President, Stressing Economic Gains, Warns of 'Snake-Oil Cures,' " *New York Times*, 12 April 1984, 2:13.

7. Steven V. Roberts, "The President's Hard Sell on Free Trade," *New York Times*, 29 September 1985, 4:1.

8. "Tariffs Seen Losing Support," *New York Times*, 9 March 1987, 4:4.

9. Clyde H. Farnsworth, "Counting Ways to Open—And Close—Markets," *New York Times*, 9 March 1987, 1:1.

10. For an assessment of the growing influence of the media on the rhetorical presidency, see Theodore Windt, "Presidential Rhetoric: Definition of a Discipline," in *Essays in Presidential Rhetoric*, ed. Theodore Windt and Beth Ingold, 2nd ed. (Dubuque, IA: Kendall/Hunt Publishing Co., 1987), and James W. Ceaser, Glen E. Thurow, Jeffrey Tulis, and Joseph M. Bessette, "The Rise of the Rhetorical Presidency," *Presidential Studies Quarterly*, 11, no. 2 (Spring 1981), 158–171.

11. Ronald Reagan, "International Trade: Remarks to Business Leaders and Members of the President's Export Council and the Advisory Committee for Trade Negotiations," 23 September 1985. All presidential remarks are taken from the *Weekly Compilation of Presidential Documents (WCPD)* unless otherwise noted.

12. Ibid.

13. David Shribman, "Trade Official's Message: 'Start Competing,' " *New York Times*, 17 March 1982, 2:20.

14. Ronald Reagan, "Remarks to Harley-Davidson Employees," *WCPD*, 6 May 1987.

15. Harry Bacas, "The Two-Front Fight on Trade," *Nation's Business*, September 1985, 30.

16. Richard B. McKenzie, "America's Competitiveness—Do We Really Need to Worry?" *Public Interest*, 90 (Winter 1988): 67.

17. Ronald Reagan, "International Free Trade," *WCPD*, 20 November 1982.

18. Ronald Reagan, "Japan–United States Trade Relations/Free Trade," *WCPD*, 25 April 1987.

19. Ibid.

20. Ronald Reagan, "Protectionism," *WCPD*, 31 August 1985.

21. Reagan, "Japan–United States Trade Relations."

22. Ronald Reagan, "National Association of Manufacturers, Remarks at the Association's Annual Congress of America Industry," *WCPD*, 29 May 1986.

23. Clyde F. Farnsworth, "President to Ask Congress to Help with a Trade Plan," *New York Times*, 7 September 1985: 1:1.

24. Robert W. Merry, "Reagan's Aides Split Over His Trade Speech and Altered It Sharply," *Wall Street Journal*, 24 September 1985, 1:12.

25. Reagan, "International Trade."

26. Ibid.

27. Ibid.

28. Reagan, "National Association of Manufacturers."

29. For an analysis of Reagan's rhetorical divisions between the United States and the Soviet Union, see Beth A. J. Ingold, "Ideology, Rhetoric, and the Shooting Down of KAL007," in *Essays in Presidential Rhetoric*, ed. Theodore Windt and Beth Ingold, 2nd ed. (Dubuque, Iowa: Kendall/Hunt Publishing Co., 1987), 415–428.

30. Reagan, "Japan–United States Trade Relations."

31. Ibid.

32. Reagan, "National Association of Manufacturers."

33. Ronald Reagan, "The Nation's Farmers, Radio Address to the Nation," *WCPD*, 14 September 1985.

34. Ronald Reagan, "Remarks at the Annual Meeting of the Board of Governors, World Bank Group and International Monetary Fund," *WCPD*, 27 September 1985.

35. Reagan, "International Free Trade."

36. Reagan, "Remarks at the Annual Meeting of the Board of Governors."

37. Reagan, "National Association of Manufacturers."

38. Philip Wander, "The Rhetoric of American Foreign Policy," *Quarterly Journal of Speech*, 70, no. 4 (November 1984): 343.

39. Ibid., 349.

40. Clyde H. Farnsworth, "U.S.-Japan Trade Showdown," *New York Times*, 27 March 1982, 1:29.

41. Steven V. Roberts, "In Ohio, the Enemy Is Japan," *New York Times*, 25 April 1982, 3:8.

42. Ibid.

43. "The Momentum Builds for Protectionism," *Business Week*, 4 October 1982, 44.

44. Clyde H. Farnsworth, "West and Japan Promise to Avoid Trade Restraints," *New York Times*, 17 January 1982, 1:1.

45. Clyde H. Farnsworth, "The Drive Is on to Change the Rules," *New York Times*, 7 November 1982, 3:25.

46. Reagan, "International Trade."

Similar to President Reagan, Bush kept trade off of the public agenda with the notable exception of the Asian trip. For the balance of his administration, trade policy consisted of minimizing protectionist pressures via fair trade measures while negotiating for free trade through international trade pacts, with GATT and NAFTA the most prominent. Also following in the tradition of the Reagan presidency in using the network news to its rhetorical advantage, the Bush administration presented itself as fighting for fair trade abroad through appropriate displays such as visuals of President Bush at international economic summits and using American manufacturing plants as backdrops for presidential proclamations on the strength of the economy.

President Bush's promotion of free trade was largely confined to segments in major addresses on global domestic and foreign issues. The 1990, 1991, and 1992 State of the Union Addresses were major speeches in which Bush articulated his policy on trade. In addition, Bush used the traditional presidential forum of universities to discuss foreign policy, including international economics.

In President Bush's conception of the new world order, trade—although an integral component of foreign policy—was not rhetorically potent. Free trade was an ideal to be emulated as the basis of a capitalist economy and a democratic polity, not a policy to be closely examined in a new era of economic interdependence and increasingly managed trade. It was an issue most notably in two areas: the trade deficit and the international trade pacts, NAFTA and GATT. The trade deficit put the administration on the defensive. The trade pacts, although administration initiatives, were primarily private, persuasive campaigns, even when economics came to the forefront in the 1992 presidential campaign. Again similar to Reagan, Bush made trade pronouncements only to affected partisan audiences and surrounding international trade summits.

From the outset of his administration, President Bush reaffirmed his commitment to free trade and free markets. In his inaugural address, Bush proclaimed: "We know what works: Freedom works. We know what's right: Freedom is right. We know how to secure a more just and prosperous life for man on Earth: through free markets, free speech, free elections, and the exercise of free will unhampered by the state."[5]

In his 1990 State of the Union Address, Bush acknowledged that the new political circumstances of the post–Cold War era had resulted in heightened economic competition. Thus, domestic economic adjustments were necessary: "In the tough competitive markets around the world, America faces the great challenges and great opportunities. And we know that we can succeed in the global economic arena of the nineties, but to meet that challenge, we must make some fundamental changes—some crucial investment in ourselves."[6]

In advocating investment, Bush was consistent with previous administrations—both Republican and Democratic. The distinction between the parties was in emphasis. For example, while disavowing managed trade, Bush accepted the realities of the international marketplace while upholding the ideal of free trade: "I still believe that free markets work. I know that there is no such thing as pure free trade in the world today, but we believe in free trade, and obviously in fair trade as well."[7]

However, in his personal politics emphasizing foreign policy, President Bush was careful to define trading partners as allies in the economic marketplace. Doing so disallowed a zero-sum definition of trade with clear winners and losers: "Our trade relationships are a vital factor in America's international alliances that help secure freedom and stability for so much of the world. We will apply firmness to help promote what is fair, but we will always remember that our major trading partners are not our enemies but, indeed, they are our allies."[8]

President Bush recommitted the United States domestically to the ideal of the free market, and in doing so nullified the Democrats' desire for government intervention. As emerging nations chose democracy, America was obligated to continue promoting its stellar model of economic freedom: "As the world turns to freer markets—and you're seeing this happen, some solidifying their commitment to freer markets, countries that never had the benefit of free markets—but as the world moves in this direction, this is not time to become wishy-washy about where America stands. The jury is no longer out. Markets work. Government controls do not work."[9]

Republican conservatism dictated a rhetoric of free trade in principle; allowing, yet rhetorically minimizing, fair trade in practice. However, in the post–Cold War era, presidents must promote free trade, which is vital to international economic growth, while more aggressively protecting domestic economic interests against unfair trading practices.[10] President Bush did so through his emphasis on reciprocity, whereby he defined his administration's capitulations to managed trade as consistent with an export-led trade policy: "The goal of this administration's trade policy, simply put, is to open markets, not close them; to fight protectionism, not to give in to it. We don't want an America that is closed to the world. What we want is a world that is open to America. We're going to work to promote American exports and to see to it that in dealing with the United States other nations play by the rules."[11]

Opening markets through fighting for fair trade propelled negotiations—multilateral and bilateral—to the forefront of administration trade policy. Throughout his presidency, Bush emphasized the importance of concluding the GATT Uruguay Round: "The Uruguay round of the GATT continues to be the centerpiece of our trade strategy. While the lack of effective multilateral rules and enforcement mechanisms has forced us to resort to section 301 [a mandatory imposition of tariffs in response to unfair trading practices of foreign nations], we look forward to the day when such actions will be unnecessary."12

True to the ideal of free trade, President Bush portrayed as regrettable actions the United States had taken to ensure fair trade. Strategically, these maneuvers were economically defensible, but rhetorically, his language undermined the image of a strong executive aggressively protecting U.S. domestic economic interests. Moreover, the Bush administration's pursuit of bilateral and multilateral trade agreements further promoted the perception of cooperation with trade partners who openly ignored fair trade rules.

The Bush administration, in striving for consistency in adhering to the principle of free trade, downplayed unilateral actions taken to punish erring trading allies and protect U.S. domestic interests despite the reality that unilateral actions were integral to the administration's trade policy. Politically and rhetorically, such actions were defensive. The Omnibus Trade and Competitiveness Act of 1988 forced the administration to name and act on unfair traders through the "Super 301" provision. For example, on 26 May 1989 the administration named three unfair traders: Japan, India, and Brazil. Nonetheless, President Bush stressed cooperation with allies and adherence to the principle of free trade when announcing this action, thus undermining any aggressive tone in regard to protecting U.S. interests: "Our goal is to open markets and to eliminate trade barriers. We oppose protectionism in any all forms. Therefore, I urge the Governments of Japan, India, and Brazil to work with us to resolve these issues expeditiously."13 Announcing the extension of voluntary restraint arrangements on steel on 25 July 1989, Bush again stressed the ideal of free trade despite the existence of unfair trade practices:

Today I am emphasizing a Steel Trade Liberalization Program that will extend for 2½ years the voluntary restraint arrangements (VRAs) that limit steel imports into the United States. I am taking this step to permit the negotiation of an international consensus to remove unfair trade practices and to provide more time for the industry to adjust and modernize. This Steel Trade Liberalization Program is designed to restore free-market forces to, and end government interference in, global trade in steel.14

If President Bush had emphasized adjustment assistance, as a Democratic president might have been more philosophically inclined to do, he would have promoted the image of the president as protector of the national interest. Bush's chosen emphasis on the ideal of free trade would have been more suitable in an atmosphere of public confidence in the growth of the domestic economy and the perception that trading partners were mending their ways. However, in an atmosphere of continued foreign promises—most notably, by Japan—of opening markets despite the continuation of closed markets, emphasizing a commitment to the principle of free trade only perpetuated an image of the United States as a patsy. In an era of rebuilding following World War II, trade policy was an economic tool closely aligned with political proclivities, attested to by such devices as the Marshall Plan and the dictum, "trade, not aid." As foreign nations rebuilt their economies and became economic competitors with the United States, economic policies once deemed vital to U.S. political security became outmoded and, indeed, harmful to U.S. domestic industries. Nowhere was this more evident than in U.S. policy towards Japan.

In summary, President Bush's rhetoric emphasizing the importance of free trade while allowing for fair trade in response to predatory foreign nations was defensive in tone, as well as in practice. In addition, unlike Reagan, who relied on the rhetorically potent symbol of Smoot-Hawley and consistent antiprotectionist metaphors, Bush used no potent rhetorical symbols. One of his few uses of metaphor occurred in a 1989 address to the United Nations. It, too, emphasized export-led growth and, more important, attempted to combat the perception that beneficial trade required reciprocity: "The free market and its fruits are not the special preserve of a few. They are a harvest that everyone can share."[15] While Bush defined free trade according to the theory of comparative advantage, in which all parties would benefit from open markets, the public viewed trade as a zero-sum game, in which there were clear winners and losers. Moreover, Bush's definition of free trade as fair trade reflected the zero-sum perception, as did his correlated trade policy of unilateral actions.

President Bush's rhetoric on trade policy was affected by both his preference for foreign policy and his assessment of the state of the Cold War. It was not until he accepted the dissolution of the Soviet Union and recognized domestic discontent with the economy that he was ready to shift his focus to the latter. Bush did not share President Reagan's enthusiasm for the Soviet Union's commitment to change in the waning years of the Reagan administration.[16] However, by 1990, Bush was ready to accept the dissolution of the Soviet Union and the end of the Cold War. In his 1990 State of the Union

Address, Bush justified his new acceptance of the post–Cold War era and the continued importance of U.S. leadership. He began to define what the momentous events of 1989—Panama, Poland, Czechoslovakia, and the Berlin Wall—meant for U.S. domestic policy: "In the tough competitive markets around the world, America faces the great challenges and great opportunities. And we know that we can succeed in the global economic arena of the nineties, but to meet that challenge, we must make some fundamental changes—some crucial investment in ourselves."[17]

Rhetorically, President Bush was making an important transition. He was moving beyond merely emphasizing reciprocity to the internal requirements for meeting the demands of increased economic competition from abroad. Bush proposed investment in physical, intellectual, and human capital; a Family Savings Plan; cutting the capital gains tax; increased research and development; drug prevention; space exploration; and education. With the exception of cutting the capital gains tax, this was a bipartisan agenda. Through focusing on domestic improvements, Bush was able to preserve a positive economic outlook despite the increasing trade imbalance. Bush echoed Reagan's optimism in arguing that such investment would preserve America's ability to compete—and issued a challenge to the American workforce: "These investments will keep America competitive. And I know this about the American people: We welcome competition. We'll match our ingenuity, our energy, our experience and technology, our spirit and enter-prise against anyone. But let the competition be free, but let it also be fair. America is ready."[18]

While Bush's trade rhetoric was evolving, his policy was not. Even in 1991, true to the Republican ideal of limited government and the free market, Bush did not advocate intervention in the economy despite the recession: "We will get this recession behind us and return to growth soon."[19] In addition, Bush continued to emphasize commitment to interna-tional organizations: the Uruguay Round of GATT, a Mexican free trade pact, and the Enterprise for the Americas Initiative (EAI). While the strengthening of multilateral institutions was critical to liberalized trade and international economic interdependence, presidential commitment to such a strategy was, ironically, close to appeasement domestically. For as long as the public's perception was foreign nations violating the rules of free trade, continued U.S. adherence to these very same rules was pure folly. President Bush's continued support of fair trade heightened this contradic-tion by reinforcing the perception of an ineffectual multilateral structure. It was thus rhetorically advantageous for the Bush administration to pursue a largely private persuasive campaign for passage of the North American Free Trade Agreement (NAFTA).

NEGOTIATING NAFTA: A PRIVATE CAMPAIGN

President Bush chose a rhetorical strategy of speeches to select audiences affected by the proposed NAFTA agreement. NAFTA and Latin American trade policy were not focal points for the Bush administration. It was Japan, Asia, and Europe that most often commanded attention in trade. Even when announcing major policy initiatives, such as NAFTA and the Enterprise for the Americas Initiative, Bush continued his policy of making select speeches to affected audiences only. Moreover, it was politics, not economics, that was the primary determinant of U.S. policy toward Mexico and Latin America during the Bush administration. The United States was most concerned with the political stability of its neighbors to the south. While in the long run, free trade with Latin America would benefit the United States, the political capital necessary to achieve a trade agreement was not warranted by the short-term economic benefits. Nonetheless, the promotion of free trade corresponded with the Bush administration's governing philosophy: its adherence to free markets and the democratic principles implied. It was thus advantageous for the Bush administration to promote free trade agreements without prioritizing their passage. Select protectionist measures, which were often punitive, remained the mainstay of U.S. trade policy.

In this respect, President Bush's trade policy was, in essence, a continuation of President Reagan's policy. The impetus for NAFTA can, in fact, be traced directly to Reagan. When announcing his candidacy for the presidency in 1979, Reagan called for the negotiation of a trade agreement between the United States, Canada, and Mexico: "A developing closeness between the United States, Canada, and Mexico would serve notice on friend and foe alike that we were prepared for the long haul, looking outward again and confident of our future; that together we are going to create jobs, to generate new fortunes of wealth for many and provide a legacy for the children of each of our countries."[20] The idea of a hemispheric free trade zone can be found in President Reagan's trade rhetoric. For example, when briefing business leaders on the United States-Canada free trade agreement, Reagan pledged to extend free trade agreements to Mexico and Latin America: "We will, together with our new partner in peace and freedom, Canada, carry the banner of free trade to Mexico, to the Caribbean, and all of Latin America—and from there on around the world."[21]

While NAFTA was initially proposed by the Reagan administration, it was the Bush administration that nurtured the pact and announced the Enterprise for the Americas Initiative—enveloping NAFTA in the womb of Western Hemispheric Free Trade Agreement (WHFTA), to ultimately create a thirty-three nation trading bloc. Herein lay the problem for the Bush administration. President Bush did not aggressively pursue conclusions to trade agreements, yet in his trade rhetoric, he persisted in shifting America's next battleground from military to economic competition. When he publicized this struggle during election campaigns, however, he only highlighted his administration's failure of both domestic and international leadership. Bush's letter to Congress transmitting NAFTA, on 18 September 1992, exemplified the rhetorical landmines in his administration's trade strategy:

Just as America prevailed in the Cold War, we must continue to lead the world in the global economy of the next century. Exports are vital to the health of the U.S. economy, accounting for 70% of our economic growth since 1988 and supporting the jobs of more than 7.5 million Americans. We must continue to expand our exports by strengthening our lead in technological innovation, by giving American firms and workers to tools to compete and win in international competition, and by negotiating effective agreements to open foreign markets to U.S. goods and services.[22]

When President Reagan rooted his trade rhetoric in an optimistic vision of an expanding U.S. economy, it seemed plausible given renewed economic vigor. When President Bush attempted the same feat amid the recession of the early 1990s, it only served to underscore his administration's domestic economic failures.

Recognizing the tendency of past administrations, including his own, to proclaim the importance of trade while publicly neglecting trade policy, President Bush stressed that his administration would aggressively seek agreements and not just rely on empty rhetoric: "I don't want this Enterprise Initiative to be just more rhetoric; we want action. This President wants action. But the climate for this kind of action is so much better today that I think we will be successful to go along the course we've been discussing here. We're [in] different times, different times."[23]

However, aggressively seeking agreements was not equivalent to placing trade pacts high on the public agenda. When President Bush did speak on trade with Latin America, he made two primary arguments: first, he placed initiatives in the context of the "new world order," and second, he assuaged domestic concerns over jobs and the environment. The former argument focused on adherence to the principle of free trade; the latter focused on the consequences of free trade.

The Context of the New World Order

President Bush, in promoting NAFTA and EAI, was proposing a new direction in U.S. trade policy. Because he was advocating free trade in an economy with a significant protectionist element, placing such actions in a new situation—the context of the new world order-was critical. Therefore, in speeches on Latin American trade policy, Bush consistently made adhering to the principle of free trade in the changing world order his first argument. In June 1990, he announced EAI in these terms: "Nations are turning away from the statist economic policies that stifle growth and are now looking to the power of the free market to help this hemisphere realize its untapped potential for progress. A new leadership has emerged, backed by the strength of the people's mandate, leadership that understands that the future of Latin America lies with free government and free markets."[24]

Announcing the successful conclusion to NAFTA negotiations on 12 August 1992, President Bush immediately placed the agreement in historical context: "The Cold War is over. The principal challenge now facing the United States is to compete in a rapidly changing and expanding global marketplace."[25] Bush was attempting to create an alternate foreign policy paradigm to replace the Cold War bipolarism, yet in doing so, he was replacing one form of competition with another. He continued to ground economic competition in the abstract principle of free trade and free markets, thus opposing the United States to any country not adhering to the free market and democratic tradition.

Bush connected economic freedom with political freedoms. In his rhetoric, because Latin America was assuming democratic political responsibilities, it deserved economic responsibilities: "Throughout the region, nations are turning away from the statist economic policies that stifle growth and are now looking to the power of the free market to help this hemisphere realize its untapped potential for progress. A new leadership has emerged backed by the strength of the people's mandate-leadership that understands that the future of Latin America lies with free government and free markets."[26]

Promoting further economic agreements with Chile on 13 May 1992, President Bush reaffirmed the connection between economic and political freedoms: "Chile has married a free people with free markets—a union that has resulted in faster economic growth than any other economy in Latin

America over the last decade."[27] Yet Bush needed to reconcile bilateral and multilateral trade agreements with both seemingly aggressive trading actions by foreign nations and the principle of free trade, in which trade agreements would be of limited importance given the theoretical advantage of unilateral free trade.

First, Bush expressed his administration's continued commitment to the Uruguay Round: "The successful completion of the Uruguay Round remains the most effective way of promoting long-term trade growth in Latin America and the increased integration of Latin nations into the overall global trading system."[28] Second, Bush explained that his administration would seek intermediate trade agreements while seeking the long-term goal of liberalized trade: "I understand that some countries aren't yet ready to take that dramatic step to a full free trade agreement. And that's why we're prepared to negotiate with any interested nation in the region bilateral framework agreements to open markets and develop close trade ties."[29]

However, regional trade agreements had the potential to both include favored nations and exclude others. In a statement before the Senate Finance Committee on 8 September 1992, United States Trade Representative Carla A. Hills emphasized the benefits of regional trading blocs while alluding to their exclusionary nature: "NAFTA will give U.S. companies the same competitive edge that regional trade ties give European and Japanese firms."[30] This contradiction was perhaps inevitable given the complexity of trade policy. Bilateral and multilateral trading agreements do, in some measure, conflict. However, the contradiction was made worse by the confusion in the Bush administration's rhetoric. President Bush continued to shield the pragmatic policy motives behind his promotion of NAFTA and EAI. He publicly premised these agreements on their economic benefits— which in actuality were minor. In February 1991, the International Trade Commission reported that a free trade agreement would be of only minor benefit to the United States, although its benefits would increase over time. President Bush deliberately downplayed the very real political motives of the administration, preferring instead to show it as protecting American economic interests by fighting for free trade abroad. Even more critically, Bush failed to use the rhetorical power of the presidency to garner public and congressional support for these initiatives.

Domestic Concerns: Protecting Jobs and the Environment

While the administration promoted EAI primarily abroad, the rationale for initiating the agreement was domestic: to promote free trade and expand the economy rather than contract trade through protectionism. In arguing for NAFTA, the administration emphasized its role in the creation of jobs, not its benefits of shoring up Mexico's political system or preventing default on Latin American debts.

Latin America is not critical to U.S. trading interests, accounting for only 25 percent of U.S. exports. NAFTA was of more symbolic than economic importance to the United States: "NAFTA has become a focal point in the debate over how to maintain and improve U.S. living standards in the face of stiff foreign competition and sluggish economic growth."[31]

The argument over jobs is ultimately an argument over fairness. In essence, should the United States promote free trade despite other countries' protectionist actions, resulting in short-term disadvantages for the former? Should American workers pay the price for the principle of free trade—for the extension of economic, and therefore political, prosperity as in the post–World War II period? The United States would, in all probability, lose low-wage, low-skill jobs. However, increased orders for machines, technology, and chemicals could add high-wage jobs to the U.S. economy. In this period of transition, workers who lost jobs would need retraining. This was the rhetorical dilemma for the president: the need to emphasize the positive long-term effects of liberalized trade while minimizing the short-term costs of dislocations in the workforce.

President Bush recognized the two-tiered effects of NAFTA on labor. Therefore, he emphasized that NAFTA would increase overall employment, while the administration would increase its efforts to train those temporarily displaced as trade shifted:

While NAFTA will create new, high-wage export-oriented jobs through expanded trade, we have a responsibility to ensure that all U.S. workers, including those affected by NAFTA, have the skills to compete in global markets. Accordingly, last month, I proposed a comprehensive new Federal job training program for all dislocated workers, including the relatively small number who face adjustments because of NAFTA. It will be funded at $2 billion annually—nearly triple the current budget for all of our existing worker training and assistance services.[32]

Despite Bush's minimizing of the problem of displacement and assurance that retraining would be provided, labor adamantly opposed NAFTA. Maquiladoras (foreign-owned factories in Mexico)—over 2,000 employing over 460,000 Mexicans—were the focal point for U.S. labor and environmental groups opposing NAFTA. Moreover, it was precisely the loss of jobs to low-wage Mexico that labor opposed. Democratic Senator Donald W. Riegle Jr., from the auto-producing state of Michigan, stated: "This is a jobs program for Mexico. What we need is a jobs program for America."[33] Thomas R. Donahue, secretary-treasurer of the AFL–CIO, complained: "There are 600,000 jobs along the Mexican border that used to be U.S.-based jobs."[34]

In response to maquiladoras an unusual combination of labor and environmental groups formed in opposition to NAFTA. Environmental groups decried the low environmental standards of maquiladoras, which resulted in widespread pollution. The Bush administration addressed environmental concerns: "The NAFTA contains unprecedented provisions to benefit the environment. In addition, we are moving forward with a comprehensive environmental agenda with the Government of Mexico—an agenda that NAFTA made possible."[35]

While the Bush administration made concessions to labor and environmental groups, it did not make NAFTA a prominent reelection issue. Congress, however, did. In the heat of the 1992 presidential campaign, the leading Democratic spokesman on trade, Richard Gephardt (Miss.), continued congressional pressure for additional labor and environmental safeguards: "As the agreement moves toward completion, it is becoming increasingly apparent that environmental controls, worker-adjustment policies, protections for American and Mexican workers, and incentives for American manufacturers to remain in the United States are being omitted from the draft."[36]

On 6 August 1992, the House voted unanimously (362–0) for a "sense of the Congress" resolution that it would not support any agreement that weakened U.S. health, safety, labor, or environmental laws. The House, in passing the resolution, was most concerned about sovereignty issues, as international dispute resolution panels had twice in the past year ruled that U.S. laws had violated trading agreements through restrictions on imports based largely on environmental issues. House Republicans chose to go along rather than make trade a liability for the Bush reelection campaign. David Drier, Republican from California, stated: "This resolution is much ado about nothing. I think the message needs to be made loud and clear. This in no way seeks to undermine negotiations."[37] During the reelection campaign, members of the House withheld support of NAFTA to avoid activating opposition. Representative Ed Jenkins, a retiring Democrat from Georgia, stated, "Members are worried about being blindsided in their districts."[38]

Much of the timing of NAFTA was politically motivated. Preliminary agreement on the pact by the United States, Mexico, and Canada was reached 12 August 1992, allowing an announcement prior to the Republican

National Convention on 17 August. The Bush administration hoped that NAFTA would pull votes in Texas and other Sun Belt states: "'Though Bush has made free trade a cornerstone of his re-election, he is trying to sell NAFTA primarily as a domestic initiative that will boost U.S. jobs at a time when the economy is slumping, even though administration officials concede the pact will have little immediate effect on the U.S. economy. 'Open markets in Mexico and Canada mean more American jobs,' Bush said."[39]

Domestically, Bush emphasized the creation of American jobs above all other rationales for trade initiatives: "NAFTA means exports, and more exports mean more American jobs. Between 1987 and 1991, the increase in our exports to Mexico alone created over 300,000 new American jobs. These are high-wage jobs. In the case of merchandise exports, those jobs pay workers a full 17 percent more than the average wage."[40]

In this reelection year, President Bush emphasized the powers of the office—his role as protector of the national interest in contrast to Congress's partisan instincts: "As President, only I can stand up against irrational impulses of protectionism. And as President, only I can speak for the national interests and fight for the jobs of the future."[41] However, even in this reelection year, Bush failed to aggressively seek international trading agreements. He did, however, begin to change his policy emphasis from foreign to domestic. With this change, the focus of trade policy and rhetoric also changed.

APPROACHING THE 1992 ELECTION: A REDISCOVERY OF DOMESTIC ECONOMICS

As the 1992 election approached and the recession continued, the Bush administration began to place the domestic economy on its rhetorical agenda, although it continued to emphasize other issues—character and the direction of foreign policy—in the reelection campaign. Trade remained an election year liability for Bush: "The subject of fairness in trade matters, not the esoterica of trade deficits or economic theory, is an issue with political resonance. The theme of economic nationalism—embracing education, training, technology development and getting tough on trade issues—appeals to many voters."[42] The Bush administration began to realize the depth of discontent on 5 November 1991, when former Bush attorney general and former governor of Pennsylvania Dick Thornburgh was upset by Democrat Harris Wofford in the Pennsylvania Senate race. Wofford ran on the slogan, "It's time to take care of our own." As a result of this upset, the Bush administration rescheduled a trip to Japan from November to

January and changed the trip's emphasis from national security to jobs. While Bush declared that this trip was nonpartisan with an aim of long-term economic growth, he remarked prior to departure, "I'll do what I have to do to be re-elected."[43] However, the trip was a rhetorical disaster, in which the dominant image was Bush vomiting and lying prone in the lap of the Japanese prime minister—a potent metaphor for the supplication of U.S. trading interests.

The Asian Trip: Integration of Domestic and Foreign Policy

President Bush's trip to Asia, with Japan as the centerpiece, is a microcosm of his administration's trade policy. Bush retained the executive emphasis on free trade while adjusting to domestic pressures by stressing fair trade in an export-oriented policy. The original purpose of the trip was security concerns in the post–Cold War era, culminating in the Tokyo Declaration affirming the importance of the U.S.-Japanese alliance. When the administration refocused the trip, it moved trade to the forefront of its agenda and began to integrate domestic economic politics into its former foreign trade policy emphasis.

The pressures on the executive to prioritize domestic over foreign policy on intermestic issues, the tendency of the more protectionist Congress to threaten trade-restricting bills, and the complementary tendency of the executive to wield such threats to pressure foreign governments were in sharp focus in the rhetorical exchanges surrounding this trip. Consistent with his rhetorical emphasis on process, President Bush explicitly commented on the traditional executive-congressional dance on trade policy: "I think it's ridiculous to start throwing in special legislation just before a trip to kind of look like the macho trying to dictate the foreign policy of this country. It's crazy. But they have their own constituents, and I've got mine. But it's all good-spirited, and we'll do our thing, keep it on broad international principles, and then take my case to the American people."[44]

President Bush emphasized his commitment to the principle of free trade, as well as his efforts to enforce the rules of fair trade, with his presidential responsibility to do this while balancing security concerns. In an official statement made upon departure, Bush highlighted the role of the executive in promoting and connecting foreign economic prosperity, domestic economic success, and political security:

In this new world, old notions no longer apply. The sharp lines that once separated foreign and domestic policy have been overtaken by a new reality. If we want to put people to work here at home, we've got to expand trade and to open markets. These new economic realities have not eclipsed the security concerns that continue to demand our attention. Our Asian/Pacific friends will play a crucial role in helping us build a post–Cold War world defined by prosperity and trade, not poverty and isolationism.[45]

In his less formal remarks, President Bush reiterated his new emphasis on American jobs: "But let me make very clear the focus of this trip. My highest priority is jobs, and I want us to build a foundation for sustained economic growth and an ever-increasing supply of good jobs for American workers."[46] Emphasizing jobs meant emphasizing open markets and fair trade: "Here at home, all of us are concerned about our sluggish economy. One way to get this economy growing again is to open up markets abroad for American goods and services. The goods we make here in America, the services we provide, are second to none. More exports mean new jobs. Each billion dollars in new manufactured exports supports 20,000 new American jobs."[47]

For the first time in his presidential term, Bush was making considerable public effort to protect American interests through fighting for fair trade: "My message in each country I visit will be this: 'Free trade is a two-way street.' "[48] Yet with the rhetorical focus of the trip Japan, and the emphasis on domestic jobs and fair trade practices, the United States was the aggrieved actor on the defensive: "As President Bush sets off on his long trip through Asia, his exaggerated emphasis on jobs, jobs, and jobs is less than wise. He's trying to convey the useful point that foreign policy and the country's economic health are not separate subjects. But he's doing it in a way that encourages all the grievances and resentments against the Japanese on the part of American companies that have lost ground in competition with them."[49]

Compounding President Bush's difficulties in defining Japan as an ally—not an enemy—in trade, Japanese Prime Minister Kiichi Miyazawa attempted to justify his earlier remarks extending sympathy and compassion to the United States: "I believe the U.S. society is a great society, but there are homeless people; there is the problem of AIDs and so on. And for various reasons, education is not at high as in the past. And U.S. industries are not as company competitive as in the past for various reasons."[50]

Defending America's ability to compete accentuated these expressions of sympathy from foreign nations, which reinforced Americans' resentment of foreign nations. Emphasizing the need to expand markets highlighted unfair trading practices. Choosing corporate executives, the first ever to accompany a U.S. president overseas, was a gesture of symbolic significance intended to showcase U.S. economic successes, but instead, it highlighted American management deficiencies.

A combination of circumstances refocused the trip to the president's disadvantage. On 8 January, the eve of his major address in Japan, Bush, who had been weakened by the flu, vomited and collapsed into the lap of the Japanese prime minister. Immediately the focus of the trip became the president's health. Expressions of sympathy from the Japanese hosts only magnified their earlier complaints about American workers, management, and the state of the U.S. economy, which served to underscore their attitude of economic superiority. Returning to the United States, Bush was met with the report of higher unemployment figures—7.1 percent, the highest in five years. He attempted to define these numbers as a temporary setback, which was reversible given the administration's fight to open markets and thus create jobs:

In each country on this mission we made progress on a top priority of this trip, renewing the strength of the American economy and generating world economic growth. Now, while I'm disappointed that the unemployment numbers went up in December here, our work over the last few days will help open markets for American companies and provide more jobs for our workers. Make no mistake about it, our progress this week will translate into progress on jobs and economic growth in America. The results will be clear and measurable.[51]

However, in a *USA Today* poll, 56 percent of Americans did not believe the trip would produce more domestic jobs, while only 28 percent thought it would.[52] A *Wall Street Journal*/NBC poll found that only 19 percent of Americans blamed Japan for America's economic problems, while 53 percent blamed American management and labor.[53]

Further undercutting the president's attempts to portray the trip as a success, auto executives, in statements upon their return, attempted to further resentment against the Japanese. On the day of Bush's return, Chrysler chairman Lee Iacocca fumed: "I for one am fed up hearing from the Japanese, and I might say some Americans too, that all our problems in this industry, all our problems, are our own damn fault. We do not have idiots running General Motors, Ford, and Chrysler, or our suppliers. And our workers are not lazy and stupid."[54]

As if to answer, and inadvertently justify, Iacocca's remarks, President Bush began a series of speeches on the strength of the American workforce. In doing so, he appropriated President Reagan's use of factories as visual backdrops of American economic strength. For example, at the Stryker

Corporation in Michigan, Bush echoed Reagan's optimistic rhetoric about the ability of the American workforce: "Don't tell me the American worker can't compete with the Japanese. You're solid proof that when the playing field is level, when you have access to the other guy's market, American workers can outthink, outperform, and outproduce anyone, anyplace in the world."[55] However, in emphasizing American workers' ability to compete in a fair market, he was contradicting his earlier rhetoric emphasizing cooperation with the Japanese and the inroads American imports had made into the Japanese market.

This inconsistent rhetoric continued in President Bush's remarks at the NAFTA initializing ceremony held less than one month before the election. While emphasizing his presidential role as protector of the national interest, Bush refuted the two primary arguments against the international trade pact: "As President, only I can stand up against irrational impulses of protectionism. And as President, only I can speak for the national interest and fight for the jobs of the future."[56] This promotion of free trade conflicted with the administration's attack on unfair trade. However, fair trade was more potent rhetorically, capitalizing on economic nationalism: "Americans are one of the only—if not the only—people in the world who imagine themselves to have a global mission. Successful competition from other nations threatens this sense of national uniqueness and destiny."[57]

Emphasizing Fair Trade

In the 1992 election campaign, the administration emphasized the fair in free trade, relegating NAFTA to private congressional persuasive campaigns. NAFTA surfaced in a congressional vote over extending "fast track" negotiating authority for the executive branch on trade treaties. This translated into a straight up-or-down congressional vote on trade pacts, with no possibility for amendments. Opponents assailed this as an unwarranted delegation of legislative authority to the executive branch. Bush countered that fast track authority was essential to the administration's ability to negotiate in good faith: "A vote against the extension of Fast Track authority would cut off the chance to negotiate any new agreements. Simply put, a vote against Fast Track is a vote against trade, against ourselves, against our neighbors."[58] The administration was successful. The House and Senate extended Fast Track authority in May 1991.

However, this victory was not easily translatable into a victory for free trade and U.S. economic interests, for pressing for international trade agreements with increased executive authority was not advantageous for either Congress or the president. The administration's negotiation of bilateral trade agreements with Canada and Israel, were similarly, not rhetorical successes. Even the Administration's trade priorities—NAFTA and the extension of GATT—were rhetorically minimized, even more so because passage failed to come during Bush's administration. The logistics of trade policy are complicated and do not easily convert into rhetorical successes. This problem is endemic to trade politics for any executive. Highlighting trade activates the protectionist public. The benefits of free trade are long-term and diffuse, while the immediate consequences of fair trade are readily apparent, thus activating the vocal few. The arcane details of trade agreements are no match for the persuasive potency of protectionist arguments. Therefore, although in what is most vital to American economic growth, the continued liberalization of international trade, the Bush administration was successful, this advancement of U.S. interests was rhetorically invisible.

In the 1992 presidential campaign, both Democratic and Republican candidates sounded remarkably similar in calling for investment, deficit reduction, and educational restructuring. In the most critical element of trade policy—promoting international economic growth through expanding free trade in international treaties—both candidates agreed. While the executive preference for free trade predominates in general election candidates, in the primaries voices of economic nationalism are more predominant: "The subject of fairness in trade matters, not the esoterica of trade deficits or economic theory, is an issue with political resonance. The theme of economic nationalism—embracing education, training, technology development and getting tough on trade issues—appeals to many voters."[59]

Therefore, it is not surprising that Bush's plan to improve the American economy—announced ten months before the election—foreshadowed Clinton's economic emphasis, including fair trade, education, investment, health care, and the deficit. There was one prominent difference between the candidates, however. Despite calling for more government involvement in the economy, Bush prefaced his call for the line item veto by decrying the size of government and thus clinging to the Republican minimalist role, stating, "The Government is too big and spends too much."[60] Meanwhile, the president was redirecting his energies toward home as was most evident in his 1992 State of the Union Address: "I mean to speak tonight of big things, of big changes and the promises they hold, and of some big problems and how, together, we can solve them and move our country forward as the undisputed leader of the age."[61] Bush directly connected the welfare of the domestic economy with the health of the global economy: "We've got to find a way to square the responsibilities of world leadership with the requirements of domestic renewal."[62] Fully embracing the role of chief executive, Bush condemned U.S. isolationism following World War I and embraced the nation's internationalism following World War II. Bush also began to rhetorically emphasis the connection between political security and economic prosperity: "We invested so much to win the Cold War. We must invest what is necessary to win the peace. If we fail, we will create new and profound problems for our security and that of Europe and Asia. If we succeed, we strengthen democracy, we build new market democracies, and in the process we create huge new markets for America."[63]

Bush explicitly connected domestic and foreign policy: "There is no distinction between how we fare abroad and how we live at home. Foreign and domestic policy are but two sides of the same coin."[64] This policy connection was an effective strategy for justifying his new policy emphasis and enabling him to counter claims of political expediency. This new emphasis was not, however, implemented into a new policy strategy emphasizing international economics. As president, Bush did not use the power of his office to aggressively seek international trading agreements. He failed to put trade high on the public agenda, and he also failed to revitalize domestic and foreign institutions as needed to reform trade policy in order to meet the demands of economic interdependence.

CONCLUSION

President Bush's rhetorical strategy on trade was reactive, consisting of promoting free, but fair, trade during election years, while in off-years, keeping trade off the public agenda. It was not until the recession became an election year liability that Bush attempted a policy change to put economic rhetoric at the forefront of his domestic agenda and integrate economic competition into his concept of the new world order. His late recognition of America's economic woes only highlighted his administration's neglect of both domestic and international economic leadership.

The Republican task is a difficult one involving reconciling the ideal of free trade, as reinforced by the executive preference for free trade, with the growing reality of fair trade and intervention in the economy. In times when the U.S. domestic economy was strong, unfair trade was not problematic. However, as the public perception of unfair trade continued with the burgeoning trade deficit and the weakening of the domestic economy, the rhetoric of free trade promoted an image of executive isolation and inaction.

George Bush's trade policy was appropriate to the demands of the executive, the tenets of free trade, and the realities of fair trade.[65] However, his rhetoric limited his ability to capitalize on this policy. For example, when Bush allowed government and industrial cooperation within the computer industry, he downplayed intervention:

Late in 1991, when the president signed legislation providing federal assistance for development of a new supercomputer, administration officials pleaded with the media for discretion. Don't call it industrial policy, one official told a *Time* magazine reporter. Call it "George Bush's incredibly forward-looking applied research and development initiatives."

The irony is that at the same time Bush was trying to cloak his policies in political euphemisms, conservative opposition to the idea of industrial policy was also beginning to dissipate.[66]

While President Bush defined free trade according to the theory of comparative advantage, in which all parties would benefit from open markets, the public viewed trade as a zero-sum game, in which there were clear winners and losers. Moreover, Bush's definition of free trade as fair trade reflected the zero-sum perception, as did his correlated trade policy of unilateral actions. Economic nationalism is also inflamed by rhetoric touting America's ability to compete while conflicting with the rhetoric of cooperation via multilateral and bilateral trade agreements. While the economic leadership role of the United States is evolving, a clearer and more consistent rhetoric asserting U.S. goals, while protecting U.S. interests, is vital.

NOTES

1. The merchandise trade deficit rose from negative $24.2 billion in 1980 to negative $118.6 billion in 1988.

2. For an explanation of the "cry-and-sigh" syndrome, see Robert A. Pastor, *Congress and the Politics of U.S. Foreign Economic Policy 1929–1976* (Berkeley: University of California Press, 1980).

3. Mortimer B. Zuckerman, "Yesterday, Today and Tomorrow," *U.S. News and World Report*, 2 December 1991, 86.

4. Selig S. Harrison and Clyde V. Prestowitz, Jr., "Pacific Agenda: Defense or Economics?" *Foreign Policy*, 79 (Summer 1990): 56.

5. George Bush, "Inaugural Address," *Weekly Compilation of Presidential Documents* (hereafter *WCPD*), 20 January 1989, 1.

6. George Bush, "Address before a Joint Session of the Congress on the State of the Union," *Public Papers of the Presidents of the United States* (Washington, D.C.: U.S. Government Printing Office, 31 January 1990), 131.

7. George Bush, "Remarks to Members of the American Retail Federation," *WCPD*, 17 May 1989, 568.

8. George Bush, "Remarks at the Swearing-in Ceremony for Carla A. Hills as United States Trade Representative," *WCPS*, 6 February 1989, 56.

9. George Bush, "Remarks to the Chamber of Commerce in Cincinnati, Ohio," *WCPD*, 12 January 1990, 43.

10. See Ethan B. Dapstein, "Workers and the World Economy," *Foreign Affairs*, 75, no. 4 (May/June 1996): 16–37.

11. George Bush, "Remarks to the American Farm Bureau Federation in Orlando, Florida," *WCPD*, 8 January 1990, 23–24.

12. George Bush, "Statement on United States Action against Foreign Trade Barriers," *WCPD*, 26 May 1989, 608.

13. Ibid., 607.

14. George Bush, "Statement on the Steel Trade Liberalization Program," *WCPD*, 25 July 1989, 1011.

15. George Bush, "Address to the United Nations," *Public Papers of the Presidents of the United States* (Washington, D.C.: U.S. Government Printing Office, 25 September 1989), 1250.

16. For an account of Bush's departure from Reagan on this score, see Sidney Blumenthal, *Pledging Allegiance* (New York: HarperCollins, 1990), 248–255.

17. George Bush, "Address before a Joint Session of the Congress on the State of the Union," *Public Papers of the Presidents of the United States* (Washington, D.C.: U.S. Government Printing Office, 31 January 1990), 131.

18. Ibid., 132.

19. George Bush, "Address before a Joint Session of the Congress on the State of the Union," *Public Papers of the Presidents of the United States* (Washington, D.C.: U.S. Government Printing Office, 29 January 1991), 76.

20. Ronald Reagan, "Remarks to Business Leaders at a White House Briefing on the Canada–United States Free Trade Agreement," *WCPD*, 4 November 1987, 1277.

21. Ibid.

22. George Bush, "Letter to Congress on North American Free Trade Agreement," *U.S. Department of State Dispatch*, 3, no. 3 (28 September 1992), 726.

23. George Bush, "Question-and-Answer Session with Reporters in Montevideo, Uruguay," *WCPD*, 4 December 1990, 1746.

24. George Bush, "Remarks Announcing the Enterprise for the Americas Initiative," *Public Papers of the Presidents of the United States* (Washington, D.C.: U.S. Government Printing Office, 27 June 1990), 874.

25. George Bush, "North American Free Trade Agreement," *U.S. Department of State Dispatch*, 3, no. 33 (17 August 1992): 641.

26. George Bush, "Enterprise for the Americas Initiative," *U.S. Department of State Dispatch,* 1, no. 1 (3 September 1990): 48.

27. George Bush, "U.S.-Chilean Relations," *U.S. Department of State Dispatch*, 3, no. 20 (18 May 1992): 387.

28. George Bush, "Enterprise for the Americas Initiative," 49.

29. Ibid.

30. Carla A. Hills, "The North American Free Trade Agreement: A Promise Fulfilled," *U.S. Department of State Dispatch,* 3, no. 37 (14 September 1992): 697.

31. David S. Cloud, "Will NAFTA Prove a Policy Prophecy?" *Congressional Quarterly,* 26 September 1992, 2893.

32. George Bush, "Letter to Congress on North American Free Trade Agreement," *U.S. Department of State Dispatch,* 3, no. 39 (28 September 1992): 726.

33. David S. Cloud, "Bush Says Free-Trade Pact Promises Growth, Jobs," *Congressional Quarterly* (15 August 1992), 2437.

34. Ibid.

35. Bush, "Letter to Congress."

36. David S. Cloud, "Democrats Renew Pressure on Free-Trade Pact," *Congressional Quarterly,* 1 August 1992, 2258.

37. John H. Cranford, "House Signals Concerns on Free-Trade Pact," *Congressional Quarterly,* 8 August 1992, 2334.

38. David S. Cloud, "Free-Trade Pact Buffeted by Election-Year Forces," *Congressional Quarterly,* 12 September 1992, 2699.

39. Cloud, "Bush Says Free-Trade Pact Promises Growth."

40. George Bush, "Remarks at the Initialing Ceremony for the North American Free Trade Agreement in San Antonio, Texas," *WCPD,* 7 October 1992, 1877.

41. Ibid., 1882.

42. Steve Lohr, "Blaming Japan Has Its Risks; So Does Bush's Visit to Tokyo," *New York Times,* 4 January 1992, 4:1.

43. Michael Duffy, "Mission Impossible," *Time,* 20 January 1992, 14.

44. George Bush, "The President's News Conference with Prime Minister Keating of Australia in Canberra," *WCPD,* 2 January 1992, 15.

45. George Bush, "Remarks Upon Departure for Asian/Pacific Nations," *WCPD,* 30 December 1991, 1.

46. Ibid.

47. Ibid.

48. Ibid.

49. "Mr. Bush in Asia," *Washington Post,* 2 January 1992, A22.

50. Kiichi Miyazawa, "The President's News Conference with Prime Minister Miyazawa of Japan in Tokyo," *WCPD,* 9 January 1992, 65.

51. George Bush, "Remarks and an Exchange with Reporters on Arrival from Asian/Pacific Nations," 10 January 1992, 67–68.

52. E. J. Dionne Jr. and Howard Kurtz, "Bush's Opponents Denounce Japan Trip as Failure," *Washington Post,* 11 January 1992, A1.

53. John Schwartz et al., "The Push to 'Buy American,' " *Newsweek,* 3 February 1992, 33–35.

54. Michael Wines, "Bush Returns, Hailing Gains in Japan Agreement," *New York Times,* 11 January 1992, A1.

55. George Bush, "Remarks to the Stryker Corporation Employees in Kalamazoo, Michigan," *WCPD*, 13 March 1992, 468.

56. George Bush, "Remarks at the Initializing Ceremony for the North American Free Trade Agreement in San Antonio, Texas," *WCPD*, 7 October 1992, 1872.

57. Michael Prowse, "Is America in Decline?" *Harvard Business Review* (July–August 1992), 37.

58. George Bush, "Remarks at a White House Briefing for the National Leadership of the Hispanic Alliance for Free Trade," *WCPD*, 19 March 1991, 286.

59. Lohr, "Blaming Japan."

60. George Bush, "Address before a Joint Session of the Congress on the State of the Union," *Public Papers of the Presidents of the United States* (Washington, D.C.: U.S. Government Printing Office, 28 January 1992), 156.

61. Ibid.

62. George Bush, "Remarks at the Richard Nixon Dinner," *Public Papers of the Presidents of the United States* (Washington, D.C.: U.S. Government Printing Office, 11 March 1992), 429.

63. Ibid., 430.

64. Ibid., 431.

65. During President Bush's administration, the merchandise trade deficit declined from a negative $109.6 billion (in 1989) to a negative $84.5 billion (in 1992).

66. Kevin P. Phillips, "U.S. Industrial Policy: Inevitable and Ineffective," *Harvard Business Review* (July–August 1992): 108.

Chapter Five

President Clinton Engages Trade: Economics to the Forefront

President Clinton entered office in January 1993 primed to focus on the economy, as befitting the first Democratic president in twelve years facing a continuing, albeit slightly improving, recession. While Clinton's domestic circumstances were dramatically different from those of his Republican predecessors, his trade policy prospects were similar: a post–Cold War political order yet to be structured by any governing paradigm.

Thus, trade policy was an executive constant. Presidents Clinton, like Presidents Reagan and Bush, had to contend with a continuing trade deficit, increased economic competition allied with increased economic interdependence, and the continued use of economic policy as a means of ensuring political alliances, all of which were at odds with a popular preference of economic nationalism. Trade therefore remained a delicate balancing act for the President, disadvantageous on the agenda yet continuing to increase in importance and receive public attention because of heightened economic interdependence.

As trade policy was evolving, President Clinton's own governing circumstances coalesced, resulting in a new emphasis in trade policy. In attempting to improve the domestic economy, Clinton again approached trade policy, this time with a renewed vigor. This was most apparent in his treatment of corresponding issues on the domestic agenda, such as governmental reform, education, and health care. Although the president continued to retain the rhetorical strategy of keeping trade off the public agenda and gave no major televised speeches on the issue, he connected trade to the domestic and foreign policy strategies necessary for invigorating the economy and securing the U.S. economic and political alliances. During his first administration, Clinton first focused on strengthening the domestic economy, then secured successful passage of NAFTA, and finally defined trade and continued competitiveness as critical to "building a bridge to the twenty-first century."

A NEW EMPHASIS: THE DOMESTIC ECONOMY

During the 1992 presidential campaign, the transition period, and throughout his first administration President Clinton established the domestic economy as his first priority. In his opening statement, prefacing the Domestic Economic Conference during the transition period, Clinton attributed his 1992 victory to Americans' dissatisfaction with "a long-term problem in the American economy as well as this prolonged recession."[1] This definition of the state of the domestic economy laid blame directly on the Republican administrations of the past twelve years for economic problems and emphasized the inherited and continuing recession. The remedy was preordained, as evidenced by Labor Secretary–designate Robert Reich's comments that Clinton's economic program would "combine short-term stimulus and job creation with a long-term attempt to reduce the federal deficit."[2] Perhaps most significantly rhetorically, however, President-elect Clinton used the conference to distinguish his administration from the Bush administration:

I called this economic conference for three reasons, first so that all of us can hear and give an assessment of where our economy is today and what has been happening to it over the last two decades. Second, so that we could bring together a diverse and talented group of Americans who make this economy work, and get your ideas and your input on how we should implement our economic plan. Third, to begin through this very public process to reconnect the American people to their government and to ask for their help too in making economic progress. I need your help and the help of every American to do what together we have to do to fulfill our obligations to ourselves and to the future.[3]

In the first two purposes, Clinton highlighted the importance of focusing on the economy—of accurate assessments and expert opinions, implying that previous administrations had ignored the input of experts, and therefore, fundamental changes in the economy. In the third rationale, Clinton highlighted the importance of the process itself: of reconnecting government to the people. Transition Chief Vernon Jordan emphasized the forum's connection to Clinton's intended public presidency: "Bill Clinton loves the discussion. If there is one result to look for, it is that the American people should feel tuned in and part of the process of dealing with the economy."4 Presidential communications Director George Stephanopolous also emphasized Clinton's intentions of reconnecting the president with the public: "The only way you can build a consensus towards solution is to make sure the people understand the scope of the problem and that they feel they are part of the solution from the beginning."5 Presidential Spokesperson Dee Dee Myers underscored Clinton's differences with Bush, namely, his recognition of the economic problems plaguing the country and, most important, the resultant effects on ordinary Americans: "One of the reasons George Bush was not re-elected is that people felt he was not connected to them, to their problems. One of the first messages Bill Clinton wants to get across is 'I get it. I understand your needs and fears. I take this seriously and I am going to work on it seriously from the first day of my Administration.' "6

Clinton advisers announced three intended audiences for the conference: Congress, business leaders, and the public.7 The array of economic experts testifying in support of Clinton's programs was intended to signal Congress that economists "shared his sense of urgency."8 At the same time, the Clinton transition team wanted to emphasize that reports of an improved economy—a decrease in the unemployment rate and an improved gross domestic product (GDP)—did not translate into a sustained economic recovery. Immediately after his election, Clinton minimized short-term improvements in economic figures: "The unemployment rate has held steady, even gone down a little bit, but the underlying reality is that unemployment is up, production is down. There are a lot of very troubling signs in the economy."9 Vice President–elect Al Gore stated, on CBS's "Face the Nation" on 13 December: "None of the figures released thus far give any reason to believe that there's been a turnaround."10 Believing that a structural economic decline would persist unless Clinton made fundamental changes in the governing of the country was critical to accepting the necessity of a more active and interventionist government. Therefore, conference participants and administration spokespeople advocated government intervention in the realm of industrial and trade policy.11

Most significant to the rhetoric of trade was the linkage between international competition and domestic policies through direct economic measures and through interrelated issues. In this conference, the implications of trade as an intermestic issue were made explicit, as domestic economic problems were linked with international economic leadership. Harold Poling, chairman and CEO of Ford Motor Company, linked escalating health care costs to international competitiveness problems: "We have reached a point where we cannot afford double digit cost increases. Our health care costs jeopardize our ability to compete, to preserve just the existing jobs, and create additional jobs."[12] Investment in people, investment in jobs, and reduction of the debt were referred to repeatedly as necessary for economic recovery. The agenda reinforced these overarching themes, on the first day focusing on the context of the global economy and then, on the second day, a discussion on restructuring government.

President-elect Clinton repeatedly emphasized the new realities of the global economy: "We are here because our nation and our people must prepare for global competition. We must revitalize and rebuild our economy."[13] He reinforced his experts' agreement on the need for an active role for government: "There is a virtual unanimous consensus that even when we disagree about what we should do, everybody acknowledges there will be very active and aggressive national government in our future, and that if we are going to have the kind of economy we want there will be some sort of partnership, for good or ill, between the public and private sector."[14]

The conference was aimed, not only at gaining public acceptance for an increased government role in the economy, but also to depict any congressional opposition as undesirable and obstructionist: "He was trying to create a political mood—a nationwide consensus that the economy is in a structural decline. He also seemed to be trying to persuade Americans that their President-elect is working on it, but that no one should expect a quick fix, and that Congress should roll over and pass whatever economic recovery program Mr. Clinton proposes."[15]

President-elect Clinton was attempting to take advantage of the honeymoon period (which had not yet officially started). It was to his advantage that he was not yet President, as it allowed him to set the agenda, free from the distractions of governing. Moreover, given the events during the first few months of his administration, during which he was sidetracked over the politically minor—but rhetorically significant—policies concerning homosexuals in the military and the hiring practices of attorney general nominees, this opportunity to control the agenda and focus on the economy was symbolically potent.

Moreover, the conference foreshadowed a pattern of the Clinton administration of attempting to educate the public as the first stage of an intense persuasive campaign. Even without the concentrated attention of the majority of the public, the central message of the conference was aptly conveyed by the national media: government needed to actively intervene in the domestic economy in order to meet the realities of global economic interdependence.

Once in office, and consistent with his emphasis on the domestic economy, President Clinton gave preference to the domestic side of trade policy in conjunction with highlighting the importance of U.S. economic leadership in the international arena. In addition, because of the greater willingness to involve government as well as the closer examination of trade policy, the Clinton administration attempted a more coordinated interagency approach.

Unlike President Bush, Clinton gave trade a prominent place on his administration's agenda, making major policy speeches at American University on 26 February 1993 and the Georgetown School of Public Affairs on 10 November 1994. In addition, Clinton gave trade policy substantial attention in his 24 January 1995 State of the Union Address. In these speeches, Clinton continued to prioritize the domestic economy and added two additional themes: the critical period of global change and the interrelatedness of domestic and foreign policy.

Consistent with the tradition of inaugural addresses, Clinton foreshadowed the governing themes of his administration. However, the new prominence of the economy and trade for the incoming administration was evident in their prominence in this speech, in the first substantive statement following the preliminary remarks: "Today, a generation raised in the shadows of the Cold War assumes new responsibilities in a world warmed by the sunshine of freedom but threatened still by ancient hatreds and new plagues. Raised in unrivaled prosperity, we inherit an economy that is still the world's strongest but is weakened by business failures, stagnant wages, increasing inequality, and deep divisions among our own people."[16]

Also in the tradition of the chief executive, Clinton called for continued American leadership internationally: "To renew America, we must meet challenges abroad as well as at home. There is no longer a clear division between what is foreign and what is domestic."[17] This statement is notable, not only for the explicit recognition of the new realities of intermestic issues, but also for the call for continued U.S. leadership in the post–Cold War period, which is similar to calls for continued U.S. leadership following World War II.

Because Clinton clearly defined trade as both a domestic and a foreign policy issue, it received a new emphasis as integral to the recovery of the domestic economy. For example, Secretary of State Warren Christopher stated, "I make no apologies for putting economics at the top of our foreign-policy agenda."[18] The rhetorical elevation of trade was manifest by the scheduling of Clinton's first foreign trip as president: to attend an economic summit that the administration labeled a "jobs summit." When President Bush had attempted the same tactic in his ill-fated trip to Japan in January 1992, he had changed the emphasis of his trip from security concerns to domestic jobs and then attempted to return to his original emphasis on security and political alliances. Moreover, a hectic schedule compounded by presidential illness further thwarted the Bush administration's attempts to control the agenda. Failure was thus not preordained by the nature of the trip. With a new administration that placed a pronounced emphasis on the economy, presidential defense of American economic interests abroad was consistent with the president's agenda.

President Clinton's emphasis on the economy was not unique nor novel. Presidents depend on a healthy economy as a basic condition for reelection. Clinton's definition of the era as a critical time of transition was not new. He would refer to the Progressive Era and post–World War II as similar times of transition; the former for economic progress, the latter for international leadership. What was new was Clinton's emphasis on the global economy in this time of transition: his treatment of trade as an intermestic issue, even with his emphasis on the domestic side of the equation. Because previous presidents had followed similar policies, albeit in different eras and with different emphases, Clinton could refer to past presidents in support of his administration's policies—a rhetorical device frequent in presidential rhetoric.

Approximately one month after his inaugural, at American University, Clinton evoked the memory of his presidential mentor, Kennedy. While President Kennedy had governed at the height of the Cold War, at American University he had proposed a new era in international relations involving a reduction in Cold War tensions. Clinton proposed a similar course, explicitly denoting the end of the era of nuclear confrontation and the beginning of the era of peaceful economic competition: "John Kennedy came to this university to address the paramount challenge of that time: the imperative of pursuing peace in the face of nuclear confrontation."[19] Clinton announced the new challenge of the post–Cold War world: "Today I come to this same place to deliver an address about what I consider to be the great challenge of this day: the imperative of American leadership in the face of global change."[20] In defining the era as a critical time of global change and in arguing for American international leadership and against isolationism, Clinton referred to the periods of change in American foreign policy following World War I and World War II—as President Bush had. However, Clinton magnified the importance of change, defining it as the "third great moment of decision in the 20th century."[21] Redefinition was essential to the presidential rhetoric of change. Emphasizing the critical need for change in an important time of transition was necessary for justifying a marked change in policy. To further his cause, Clinton charged past administrations with ignoring the new economic order and thus held them responsible for the decline of the U.S. economy. In Clinton's rhetorical worldview, the public's negative view of increased economic competition was understandable given past administrations' failures to adapt to the new economic realities of interdependence. Previous administrations had not defended American interests in fighting for free, but fair, trade. Clinton argued that he would put America first without retreating to a false isolationism:

It is ironic and even painful that the global village we have worked so hard to create has done so much to be the source of higher unemployment and lower wages for some of our people. But that is no wonder. For years our leaders have failed to take the steps that would harness the global economy to the benefit of all of our people, steps such as investing in our people and their skills, enforcing our trade laws, helping communities hurt by change; in short, putting the American people first without withdrawing from the world and people beyond our borders.[22]

Clinton acknowledged the loss of low-wage jobs as companies increasingly crossed international borders, but he presented alternatives enabling the United States to preserve domestic jobs as well as provide economic leadership. True to the executive tradition, he defended free market capitalism and engagement as opposed to isolationism, retreatism, and protectionism: "The truth of our age is this and must be this: Open and competitive commerce will enrich us as a nation. . . . And so I say to you in the face of all the pressures to do the reverse, we must compete, not retreat."[23] Clinton announced a five step plan to "set a new direction at home and to help create a new direction for the world": first, increasing investment and reducing the deficit; second, making trade a priority in U.S. security; third, exercising economic leadership among major financial powers; fourth, promoting growth in the developing world; and fifth, encouraging new democracies, especially Russia. Ensuring domestic economic prosperity was the first step in ensuring economic prosperity abroad. Clinton vowed to pursue the expansion of free trade without regard to institutional barriers: "Our trade policy will also bypass the distracting debates over whether efforts should be multilateral, regional, bilateral, unilateral."[24] Minimizing the theoretical distinctions between the levels of trade negotiations eliminated the contradictions inherent in such pursuits. It allowed the administration to pursue negotiations on NAFTA, at the Uruguay Round (multilateral negotiations through GATT), and with the Japanese without reconciling these conflicting levels of talks. Moreover, it depicted an aggressive administration trade policy actively pursuing expansion while defending U.S. interests through punishing nations that violated free trade pacts through restricting U.S. imports.

The contradictory nature inherent in a fair trade strategy—between espousing the principles of free trade while selectively restricting trade—still mitigated against placing free trade high on the public agenda. It was not until the Clinton administration was faced with a legislative battle over the North American Free Trade Agreement (NAFTA) that trade came to the forefront, for while trade policy was integral to his domestic and international economic rhetoric of meeting the challenges of the twenty-first century, trade pacts were not administration priorities. Ironically, NAFTA became one of the highlights of the Clinton administration's first term.

NAFTA: EMBRACING THE GLOBAL ECONOMY

In the fall of 1993, the Clinton administration won successful passage of NAFTA. Similar to the Kennedy administration strategy in pushing for the Trade Expansion Act of 1962, Clinton pursued a largely private campaign, going public only in a last-ditch effort to save the pact. Indeed, the administration was not sure it wanted to aggressively fight for passage of the legislation. Once again, the Democratic presidential dilemma of fighting for free trade while minimizing opposition from traditional Democratic constituencies was a delicate balancing act. Clinton was especially reluctant to publicly support NAFTA because of the vocal opposition of labor.[25] The administration deliberately avoided major public speeches in support of NAFTA, and Clinton did not personally engage the issue until September.

While a presidential candidate, Clinton used the sidebar issues of labor and the environment as excuses to avoid a public commitment on NAFTA—either for or against. Once president, Clinton continued to point to these sidebar agreements as critical conditions to his support for the trade pact. Clinton's arguments in support of NAFTA were consistent, urging bipartisanship on behalf of the national interest, long-term benefits versus short-term costs, and the importance of the pact to international competition, continued U.S. leadership, and additional trade pacts.

President Clinton used his past political experiences as grist for his current commitment to NAFTA. As a governor, he argued, he had dealt with the consequences—positive and negative—of the new global economy. Clinton used these experiences to rebut charges that he was immune to the negative consequences of plant relocation, thus personalizing his policies: "When plants closed, I knew people's names who ran the plants and worked in the plants. When people closed their plants and went to Mexico, I knew about them. And I was proud that of the three or four we lost when I was Governor, we actually brought one back before I left office. It made me feel that in part, we had squared the circle."26

Not only did his past successes as governor justify the continued expansion of free trade, but support for free trade was justified by the lessons of history. This was a typical presidential argument—with the president as educator—presenting information from the standpoint of greater knowledge and wisdom and, relying on institutional legitimacy. President Clinton pointed to historical evidence that expansion of trade was beneficial, and arguments against free trade were both familiar and erroneous:

The point I want to make is this: Anybody who has ever dealt with these issues know that most of the arguments being raised against NAFTA today are arguments being raised about economic forces and developments that occurred in the past. And anybody who has ever read the agreement knows that if you don't like it when people shut plants down and move to Mexico, that this agreement will actually make that less likely. And if we don't pass it, it will do nothing to stop what people who are complaining about it are complaining about.27

In other words, preventing passage of NAFTA would not alleviate the painful consequences of adjusting to the new economic order. Clinton immediately underscored his concern for workers who would face adjustments as a result of NAFTA but argued that in the long run, his economic policies would result in a growth in American jobs, returning in the process to a personalized rhetoric:

I would never do anything that would cost an American a job. My job is to try to recover the economic vitality of this country by working in partnership with the private sector. It is important, it is imperative that we make it clear to the American people, first of all, that you ought to look at what this agreement does: It helps to alleviate the problems that led to so many jobs moving out of our manufacturing sector, either into machines or offshore, whether to Mexico or to other places.28

President Clinton did not emphasize government-business cooperation. Accentuating public-private partnerships, though integral to Clinton's restructuring of government and the economic sector, both encroached on Republican alliances with business and evoked the specter of government intrusion in the marketplace. Clinton also did not highlight his administration's policies to ease worker dislocations: "What we're doing at the national level is to provide more money for job retraining, number one. Number two, we're going to set up a development bank to try to get funds

for indigenous businesses. And number three, we're going to have empow-
erment zones."[29]

The audience determined to a large extent President Clinton's emphasis
on worker dislocation programs, with greater attention given in speeches
before labor constituencies. Similarly, Clinton did not emphasize concessions made to protectionist forces. In trying to assuage opposition to
NAFTA, Clinton made policy concessions on sugar, citrus, and vegetables
yet minimized such actions in a necessary rhetorical strategy given the
contradiction between these protectionist actions and the free trade principles of the pact.

President Clinton referred to his executive role, not only in his explanations of acting on behalf of the national interest, but also in explaining and
thereby educating, the public on, the benefits of the trade pact. Clinton
provided a broad perspective by placing NAFTA in the context of the
worldwide expansion of trade via GATT:

I want to say to all of you that if we don't approve NAFTA, it will weaken our ability
to get a General Agreement on Tariffs and Trade passed by the end of the year. If
we do approve NAFTA, it will not only put us in a stronger position with Mexico
and with all the rest of Latin America, it will help us to say to our trading partners
in Europe and in Asia what we really need is to continue to expand trade worldwide.[30]

Clinton argued that if the United States did not negotiate a trade pact with
Mexico, Europe or Japan would. This argument directly contradicted the
economic principle of the beneficial effects of free trade internationally,
regardless of the practices of other nations. It ignored the contradictory
nature inherent in bilateral, regional, and multilateral trading pacts. Most
important, it heightened the sense of rival trading blocs—of trade policies
leading to clear winners and losers—thus exacerbating the very exclusionist
tendencies President Clinton was attempting to minimize.

In appealing to bipartisanship, Clinton made a distinction between the
secret support for NAFTA and the public pressures on Congress to vote
against their conception of the national interest: "I think if there were a
secret vote in the Congress today, we would win. Now, that's a big issue,
winning the secret ballot. I say that not to criticize anyone or to put anyone
down but to recognize that the pressures against NAFTA are enormous. But
they reflect, as I have said many times in many places, the accumulated
frustrations and grievances and insecurities people bring to this day in
American history."[31]

Clinton acknowledged that he was not impervious to the natural insecurities and fears in this time of global transition: "So there is all this uncertainty out there in America today. I understand that. And our administration has done what we could to try to alleviate the insecurities of the American working families."[32] He addressed such fears much as he had tackled the economy: focusing on domestic reforms and economic strength prior to moving to the international arena. Indeed, Clinton, as previous presidents had done, argued that expansion of export markets was essential to the American domestic economy: "With it [NAFTA], we have the prospect of having several years now of sustained, vigorous economic growth because we are getting control of our economic house; we are putting things in order; we are getting our priorities straightened out in this country; we are focusing on investment and on training. We have to have the markets."[33]

Clinton returned repeatedly to the principle that continued domestic strength was dependent on growth in the international arena. Without export markets, domestic growth would not continue: "No one attacking NAFTA has yet made a single solitary argument to refute this essential point: There is no evidence that any wealthy country—not just the United States, anyone, not one—can create new jobs and higher incomes without more global growth fueled by trade. If you strip away all the other arguments, no one has offered a single solitary shred of evidence to refute that central point."[34]

President Clinton made no major televised speech supporting NAFTA, instead continuing the presidential rhetorical strategy of making speeches on trade to select affected audiences. However, Clinton was faced with a very public foe, which changed the dynamics of the rhetorical situation. The Clinton administration had to contend with the vocal opposition of former Independent Party presidential candidate Ross Perot (who had won 19 percent of the popular vote in the 1992 election). Perot capitalized on the very uncertainties that Clinton had acknowledged and tried to minimize: the fear of loss of American jobs. Clinton continued to use his experiences in job creation while governor to refute Perot: "That one fellow talks about the giant sucking sound. I want you to understand clearly from somebody who's lived through this: This agreement will make that less likely, not more likely."[35] However, the most effective rebuttal of Perot was Vice President Gore's successful debate against Perot on the nationally televised "Larry King Live" show—a debate that was Gore's idea—for public support of NAFTA increased following telecast. This was the true benefit of the debate, which aided Clinton immensely in his attempt to sway Congress. Still,

Clinton named special interests as the force behind Congress's private and insidious opposition:

I don't consider Ross—first of all, in the Congress Ross Perot is not the primary problem we've got. The primary problem we've got in the Congress is the united, intense, and sometimes vociferous endorsements—efforts of the labor movement to beat this and to convince Republicans that they basically like, they'll get them opponents, and Democrats, if they like, they'll never give them money again. So that's the big problem we've got.[36]

Congress had to balance the interests of their respective districts with the national interest. Clinton reduced this equation, not to an issue of conflicting levels of interest, but rather to one of being beholden to special interests at the expense of the national good. Allied with this argument that NAFTA was in the best interests of the nation, Clinton relied on a presidential strategy often evocative of policies at risk for defeat—publicly enlisting the support of three previous presidents—in this case, Ford, Carter, and Bush. In both his prepared speeches and extemporaneous remarks, Clinton frequently referred to the testimony of experts supporting the pact: "41 of the 50 Governors have endorsed it—and they make their living creating jobs, keeping jobs—12 Nobel Prize winning economists, and every living former President."[37] In a final gambit, the administration scheduled the congressional vote on NAFTA immediately prior to Clinton's Asia Pacific Economic Council (APEC) meeting, in an attempt to pressure Congress to support the president prior to an important presidential summit.

However, most important to the trade rhetoric of the Clinton administration was placing NAFTA in the context of international economic leadership. Clinton echoed prior presidents in urging America to compete and win: "We cannot turn away from the global economy that is engulfing us. We know America can compete and win. We are not going to turn tail and run. We have not given up on America."[38] He recognized the symbolic importance of NAFTA, both to his administration's legislative record of success and to the opposition's rhetorical advantage in the immediate battle over passage. Clinton argued that unions that would, ironically, benefit from passage had chosen instead to portray the trade pact as symbolic of lost jobs and fallen wages: "They decided that NAFTA would be the receptacle in which all the resentments and fears and insecurities of that last 12 to 20 years of stagnant wages and economic difficulties would be poured."[39] While the administration had decided late to fully support passage of the legislation, to put the prestige of the presidency on the line it elevated the importance of passage despite the expected close vote: "It has acquired a symbolic significance for those of us who are for it, too. This is a huge diplomatic, foreign policy, and economic issue for America. You simply cannot divide domestic and foreign policy anymore, as you once could."[40]

In extemporaneous remarks in a question-and-answer period, President Clinton's use of parallelism and repetition further highlighted his belief in the importance of the pact: "So, this is a good deal for this country. And not doing it, conversely, is a very, very dangerous strategy. It's a dangerous strategy economically; it's dangerous politically. It will hurt us in the short run, and it will hurt us for 20 years. I am convinced it is a terrible, terrible mistake."[41]

In short, Clinton elevated the importance of NAFTA, defining it as a critical issue essential to economic growth in a time of transition: "NAFTA reflects this moment's expression of all the lessons we have learned in the 20th century."[42] He harked back to the Nixonian tactic of taking the route that is honorable and right, not easy and morally corrupt:

And in truth, I think when you strip all this away, we are facing a real decision about whether the psychological pressures of the moment will overcome what we know in our hearts and our minds is the right thing to do. Will those pressures make us do what is easy and perhaps popular in the moment? Or will we do what we should really do? The honorable thing to do to respond to those pressures is to take an action that may not be popular in the moment but that actually holds the promise of alleviating the pressures.[43]

As President Reagan did, Clinton equated support for trade expansion with confidence in the American spirit and ability to compete: "This is a decision which will demonstrate whether in this difficult moment we still have confidence in ourselves and our potential."[44] Clinton's support of NAFTA was consistent with his governing tome as a new Democrat and previewed his 1996 reelection theme of building a bridge to the twenty-first century: "If we embrace NAFTA, it is one strong step to take this country into the 21st century with a revitalized economy."[45] In addition, Clinton attempted to make a virtue out of a necessity, defining the administration's pursuit of bipartisan support as a measure of the worthiness of the trade pact, rather than as a sign of a divided and in fact rather unfavorable Democratic party stance: "This is clearly in the forefront of the minds of all Americans, and that is why we are pursuing it here in this bipartisan fashion."[46]

On 17 November 1993, NAFTA narrowly passed the House (234–200). There was more Democratic opposition than support, with 156 against and

102 in favor. Republicans supported NAFTA by 132 to 43. NAFTA easily passed the Senate (61–38).

With no similar chance of legislative success to support $50 billion in loans to Mexico in February 1995, the administration took executive action to rescue the Mexican economy from sure financial disaster. Originally attacked as a sign of the negative effects of NAFTA, the administration took great pains to promote the first Mexican payment on the loan ahead of schedule, publicizing the U.S. visit of Mexican President Ernesto Zedillo in October 1995.

However, the Mexican loan, which was perceived as a bailout, was indicative of the growing resentment of the public against foreign aid. While foreign aid represented only .5 percent of the budget, the public perceived foreign aid as representing 20 percent.[47] The Clinton administration attempted to correct this misconception through administration spokespeople and presidential speeches. At the time of the Mexican loan guarantee, White House Adviser Thomas McLarty emphasized the importance of multilateralism in international economics: "The IMF and the World Bank are going to have a heightened importance in the post cold-war world."[48] The morning after the loan, President Clinton stressed the domestic effects of Mexican financial stability, stating that there were "thousands of jobs, billions of dollars of American exports at stake."[49]

President Clinton had difficult circumstances to overcome in promoting free trade. Not only did he have to deal with a more protectionist Congress, a resurgence of populism, and growing isolationism, he also had to contend with the impending 1995 formation of the World Trade Organization. This body would have stronger enforcement powers that GATT, which it superceded. Thus, while the public was reverting to an isolationist position, Clinton was advocating an increased U.S. leadership role despite having less influence in multilateral economic organizations.

A CRITICAL TIME FOR GLOBAL CHANGE:
PREFACE TO THE 1996 ELECTIONS

Following the 1994 midterm elections, Clinton renewed his commitment to free trade in spite of the rise of the new Republican right and a more protectionist and isolationist Congress. The week after the election, he gave a major economic speech at Georgetown University. Clinton returned to the theme of change in a period of transition, defining the election as both a measure of voter frustration with government resulting from the unsettling pace of change: "But this is no ordinary time. And on Tuesday the voters reflected their frustration with the pace of change and the messy and often, to them, almost revolting process by which it was made."[50] He urged citizens to continue to support American economic leadership, to reject isolationism, and to continue the U.S. commitment to international economic institutions: "In this century there have been a handful of congressional votes that have demonstrated what kind of country we are and what kind of people we're going to be."[51] Clinton defined these critical votes as the League of Nations, the Marshall Plan, and, now, GATT, which he termed "the key link to free trade, more open societies, and economic growth all around this world."[52]

However, given an election interpreted as a resounding defeat for the Democratic Party and for the administration and Clinton's protest that he was, nonetheless, still relevant to the governing process, the president in essence was defending his administration's progress while announcing a redirection in course. In his 1995 State of the Union Address, he reminded voters of his administration's economic successes: "Record numbers of Americans are succeeding in the new global economy. . . . We have almost 6 million new jobs and the lowest combined rate of unemployment and inflation in 25 years."[53] Clinton attempted to assuage voter dissatisfaction by embarking on a new program—the "New Covenant": "Our New Covenant is a new set of understandings for how we can equip our people to meet the challenges of a new economy, how we can change the way our Government works to fit a different time, and, above all, how we can repair the damaged bonds in our society and come together behind our common purpose. We must have dramatic change in our economy, our Government, and ourselves."[54]

Clinton remained true to his initial governing themes of restructuring government and focusing on the economy. He had yet to coin his thematic trio of opportunity, responsibility, and community. The New Covenant was not indicative of a change in administration emphasis. Clinton remained focused on economics, reflected in the bulk of his speech summarizing Clinton's efforts to strengthen the domestic economy. On the defensive, Clinton justified the Mexican loan, American leadership internationally, and additional defense spending. He remained committed to free trade as the key means for bringing jobs to American workers, while chiding domestic businesses for shortchanging the domestic workforce—an easy target given their Republican alliances: "For our corporate and business leaders, we're going to work hard to keep bringing the deficit down, to expand markets, to support their success in every possible way. But they have an obligation when they're doing well to keep jobs in our communities and give their workers a fair share of the prosperity they generate."[55]

While Bush chose to ally himself with corporate leaders in his junket to Japan, Clinton chose to define corporate leaders as part of the problem. Hence, Clinton continued to minimize his administration's support of public-private partnerships. His support of NAFTA and GATT had antagonized labor; this was an attempt to mollify them. Attacking corporations was also one means via which Clinton attempted to meld the traditional Democratic coalitions' support for protection with this executive support for free trade. Despite his public assault on corporations, Clinton was successful in assembling bipartisan legislative support for NAFTA and GATT. The traditional stance of Democrats supporting protection and Republicans supporting free trade no longer held sway.

The administration continued to emphasize attempts to force other nations—especially Japan—to open their markets. Trade Representative Mickey Kantor stated: "For years we have allowed our workers to be hurt and our companies to be left out because we wouldn't pick up the phone and ask for the order."[56] Rhetorically, the administration emphasized the effectiveness of their diplomatic approaches to open markets. In 1995, Clinton announced:

Now in some areas we have made progress with Japan over the last 2½ years. We've concluded 14 results-oriented agreements. Believe it or not, they're now eating American rice in Tokyo. Japanese consumers are buying everything from our apples to our telecommunications equipment. But in many areas, Japan's market remains stubbornly closed. There's no question this is about artificial trade barriers, not the quality of American products.[57]

Continuing his strategy of speaking to select audiences directly affected by trade, Clinton addressed the United Auto Workers Convention and emphasized his administration's measures to open markets. Defining market-opening actions as partial successes allowed the president to indirectly transfer faith in these measures to the new measures he was announcing: "I have ordered the U.S. Trade Representative to impose 100 percent tariffs on 13 Japanese-made luxury cars by June 28 unless Japan agrees to open its markets to cars and car parts before then."[58] Clinton returned to the rhetoric of the Reagan administration in adopting the rhetoric of the playing field and fair competition: "Now we must act decisively to level the playing field and to protect American jobs."[59] However, demanding that Japan play by the rules served as a reminder of their past transgressions: "It's time for the Japanese to play by the same rules the rest of us play by. If working

Americans see us continue to put up with unfair trade deals, they'll lose their faith in open trade."[60] This, in turn, undermined the potential for success of these new trade requirements and the likelihood of imposition of penalties.

What was most remarkable about President Clinton's trade rhetoric, which is notable for both its novelty and its consistency, was his integration of economics into both his domestic and foreign policy agendas. Prefacing the themes of his 1996 reelection campaign, in his 1996 State of the Union Address Clinton described the requirements for meeting the challenges of the new global economy:

I tried to look with you into the future to describe the seven challenges our Nation will have to meet if we're going to provide the American dream for all of our people who are willing to work for it in a new, highly competitive global economy dominated by information and technology and if we're going to pull our country together here at home and, finally, if we're going to continue to lead the world for peace and freedom and prosperity.[61]

Three of these challenges were directly relevant to economic revitalization: education; jobs, health care, pensions, and lifetime training; and leading the world for peace, freedom, and prosperity.[62] In turn, Clinton folded these seven challenges into three themes: opportunity, responsibility, and community. On the campaign trail, Clinton retroactively defined past trade actions in light of these three terms. The Mexican loan became an indice of responsibility: "I think trying to help a new and responsible government in Mexico avoid bankruptcy was the responsible thing to do."[63] Responsibility also meant being a good citizen of the world: "It will be impossible in the world we're moving to—to have a clear dividing line between our domestic economic affairs and our international economic affairs, that to be an American in the twenty-first century will mean to be a citizen of the world."[64] Opportunity translated into increased educational opportunities: relevant to trade for both the high education standards necessary for competitiveness and for increasing computer capabilities in a high-tech economy. Education policy also encompassed training dislocated workers. Specifically, Clinton introduced three campaign initiatives: a G.I. bill for American workers, tax deductions for college tuition, and making the first two years of college universal.

However, the clearest demarcation of President Clinton's reelection themes and plans for his second administration was his rhetorical evocation of "building a bridge to the twenty-first century." In using this theme, President Clinton consciously evoked the anxious nature of change while reassuring the nation that they were prepared to meet such a challenge—with the right leadership: "All change is unsettling. Every change requires pain as well as bringing gain. But if we remember our mission, that we're trying to make the American dream available to everybody who will work for it, we're trying to keep our country the world's strongest force for peace and freedom, and we're trying to bring the American people together, if we remember that mission we can make the right decisions."[65]

The clearest demarcation of Clinton's re-election themes as well as his second term's goals was in Clinton's book, *Between Hope and History*.[66] Taking the form of a massive policy paper, most important, the book served as a reference point for the campaign rather than a device to persuade the undecided, who were not likely to buy or read the book. Nevertheless, the book is useful as a capsule of the campaign agenda and grand policy schemes. The themes of opportunity, responsibility, and community continued to dominate:

My vision for America at the dawn of a new century is of a nation in which the American Dream is a reality for all who are willing to work for it; our diverse American community is growing stronger together; and our leadership for peace, freedom, and prosperity continues to shape the world.

To achieve this vision we must pursue a three-part strategy. First, we must create opportunity for all Americans. Second, we must demand responsibility from all Americans. And third, we must forge a stronger American community.[67]

While the reelection campaign deliberately emphasized values and Clinton dutifully and consistently grounded his policies in opportunity, responsibility, and community, most critical to the contrast between candidates was the president's definition of the era as a time of transition: "We live in an age of enormous possibility. But it is also a time of difficult transition. As we move from the Industrial Age into the Information Age, from the Cold War to the global village, the pace and scope of change is immense."[68]

Emphasizing a time of transition and the need for new leadership underscored Clinton's youth in contrast to Republican candidate Dole's age. In defining the critical nature of change, Clinton repeatedly returned to the economic implications of specific policies: "The actions we take today will determine what kinds of jobs Americans will have tomorrow, how competitive our businesses will be in the global economy, how well prepared our children—especially the poorest among them—will be to succeed."[69] In addition to revealing his emphasis on the economy, as well as specific policies—such as education—that Clinton would highlight if reelected, defining the current period as a critical time of transition also influenced Clinton's choice of presidential role models.

The most prominent president in Clinton's rhetoric was Theodore Roosevelt, whose leadership of the Progressive movement at the turn of the twentieth century Clinton equated with the type of leadership needed during what he defined as an equivalent time of transition: "A hundred years ago, the public demanded national action to deal with the challenges rapid change created. What emerged was the Progressive Movement. It was given voice and direction by Theodore Roosevelt, a president who was committed to ensuring that the free market worked for all Americans, protecting them from the abuses of the Industrial Age, conserving the nation's natural resources, reforming government, and asserting America's leadership in the world."[70]

Although the modern citizenry was not demanding presidential action— indeed, if anything, it desired less government intrusion—President Clinton heartily embraced the theme of an active government leading the transition into the next century. He could also easily embrace the specific policies Roosevelt supported: the free market, protection from corporate abuse, conservation, the reform of government, and America's international leadership. Clinton wanted the public to adopt with him what he defined as the guiding principles of the Progressive movement, which was "about a shared vision of what America could and should be, about mending the frayed fabric of family and community, about harnessing the forces of change and using them to meet both individual dreams and common national goals. That same shared vision guides us today."[71]

As a campaign tome, *Between Hope and History* both justified past policies, defining them as successes, and assured voters that the administration would continue on their successful path:

To restore opportunity, we had to reverse escalating deficits, spur economic growth, create jobs, and give people a chance to raise their incomes. Since I took office in 1993, I have pursued a strategy for expanding opportunity with three broad objectives: first, to put the nation's economic house in order so our businesses can prosper and create new jobs; second, to expand trade in American products all around the globe; and third, to invest in our people so that they all have the tools they need to succeed in the Information Age.[72]

The economy was in good stead—in large measure leading to Clinton's reelection. However, while Clinton had success in passing trade-expanding measures—epitomized by NAFTA and GATT—the trade deficit had risen every year Clinton was in office. President Clinton was more successful in his third goal, investing in people. While the primary focus of this area was education, which fell largely under the control of states and localities, it also encompassed worker retraining, which provided an outlet for relieving trade pressures as well as a means for increasing competitiveness. Moreover, Clinton's chosen emphases—national standards, high-tech computers, and college funding-did not encroach on local control.

As reelection neared, President Clinton's trade rhetoric was even more focused on the future, in line with both his campaign focus (emphasizing a time of transition requiring innovative leadership, in contrast to Dole), and his new governing tone of maturity. Consistent with defining the era as in a critical time of change, Clinton was advocating a new vision of government: not the old Democratic welfare state, but not the more limited, Republican version, either. Clinton professed that "the era of big government is over," while defining the necessary duties of governing: "The market is a marvelous thing, but especially in a global economy, it won't give us safe streets, a clean environment, equal educational opportunities, a healthy start for poor babies, or a healthy and secure old age."[73] Thus Clinton exploited the budget impasse of the previous year, which was interpreted as a success for the administration while hurting the Republicans. Clinton defined his role in the budget battle as a principled stand for his beliefs, as defending the basic functions of government against Republican attempts to decimate Medicare and other social programs: "The Republicans believed I would give in to them just to keep government going on a lot less money. But I wasn't fighting for 'government.' I was fighting for the future of America and for a different, less bureaucratic modern approach to help people help themselves."[74]

In other words, Clinton was embracing opportunity, which he believed was the key to resolving the problems remaining in the economy and providing for smooth transitions in an era of "an economic dynamism that is inherently turbulent and disruptive."[75] Government had a precise, specific role to play in providing opportunity: "The answer to their difficulties is to get more growth, more high-wage jobs, and more education by building on the policies that have brought our economy back, with innovative, targeted practical efforts, not to abandon what we have done for a radically different course that will not help those who need it and will undermine opportunity for everyone else."[76]

The solution did not include retreating to isolationism and economic nationalism, even in an era of increasing trade difficulties. Clinton continued to acknowledge that the United States had lost low-wage jobs to other countries, while countering that the economic benefits from exports outweighed this flight. As had previous presidents, Clinton advocated a middle course, minimizing the abuses of free trade while avoiding a reactionary protectionism: "We don't need to build walls, we need to build bridges. We don't need protection, we need opportunity. But in a world of stiff competition we also need more than free trade. We need fair trade with fair rules."[77]

President Clinton defined his administration's successful conclusion of trade pacts as integral to expanding and promoting fair trade: "That's why I fought so hard for the ratification of the North American Free Trade Agreement (NAFTA), which effectively opened Mexico's and Canada's markets to American products, and for the General Agreement on Tariffs and Trade (GATT), which is helping to level the playing field for American companies abroad."[78]

Clinton promoted an active role for government in trade-expanding policies, citing administration successes in negotiating treaties and expanding exports while ignoring the burgeoning trade deficit: "In all, during the past three and a half years we have negotiated more than two hundred trade agreements—twenty-one with Japan alone. In addition, in 1993 we created America's very first National Export Strategy and, more recently, a new agricultural trade strategy."[79]

And as had previous presidents, Clinton tied economic progress to political security and alliances: "As a result of our efforts to create a new global trading system, the world isn't just a better place for Americans to do business, make money, and create jobs, it's also a safer place."[80] Clinton promoted the expansion of free markets, neglecting the more immediate concerns of human rights abuses: "That's why we have worked so hard to help build free-market institutions in Eastern Europe, Russia, and the former Soviet republics. That's why we have supported commercial liberalization in China—the world's fastest-growing market. Just as democracy helps make the world safe for commerce, commerce helps make the world safe for democracy."[81]

However, the most important integration of domestic and foreign trade emphases occurred with Clinton's proposals to ensure a trained labor force able to compete in the international arena. Economically related domestic issues both received emphasis from the Clinton administration and held the most promise for policy maneuvering: "The third part of my opportunity strategy, and in some respects the most important over the long haul, has been investing in our people and our future—in research and technology, in education and skills, and in strengthening working families."[82] Clinton again returned to focus on a state of transition necessitating fundamental changes in government policies—in this instance, federal prioritizing of education: "At critical stages in our nation's growth we have had to raise our nation's educational norms to keep up with the demands of the times."[83] Clinton's interest in education followed his actions as governor of Arkansas, as well as his leadership in the first education summit (convened by President George Bush in 1989). While Bush had also deemed education a priority, even using the moniker, "Education President," his rhetoric outstripped his actions. Clinton followed his proclamations with specific proposals, most notably Americorps (a domestic equivalent of the Peace Corps that provides college money in return for community service), a direct college loan program, and college tax credits—named "America's Hope Scholarships"—in his attempt to make the first two years of college universal. These tax credits and scholarships, which were tied to maintaining a certain grade point average, meshed with Clinton's themes of opportunity tied to responsibility: "In short, they create opportunity as long as students take responsibility."[84] Education policy was intimately related to trade. Clinton streamlined worker retraining programs—a new "G.I. Bill for America's workers"—and urged increased education standards in science, math, and other basic subjects. However, he acknowledged the federal limits in education policy, which was basically the province of state and local governments. In discussing the controversy over national standards, Clinton stated: "This has shifted the focus of standard-setting to state and local officials, who, after all, have the primary responsibility for public education in the United States."[85] Most important, though, Clinton was defining a new role for government in this era of transition. Hence, he could take the lead in education policy without preempting state and local responsibilities. He could emphasize federal programs with universal impact—such as retraining and college finance—without encroaching on state and local realms, and thus sidestep controversy, such as the issue of national standards.

President Clinton's national government was managing issues incrementally, highlighting legislation that made a daily impact on most Americans' lives, hence the emphasis on education, crime, the family leave act, and similar issues. Whether Clinton's new Democratic philosophy was centrist or adopting previously Republican policies, the president defined the party and his government as more responsible than the Republican Party yet not equivalent to the caretaker Democratic governments of the past: "We say the era of big government is over, but we must not go back to an era of 'every man for himself.' "[86] Moreover, Clinton consistently defined this new vision of government as necessitated by the new realities of economic interdependence: "There is simply no evidence that America can be better off if we abandon our attempt to go forward together and leave America's future to the tender mercies of the global marketplace."[87] Under the label of "reinventing government," Clinton stated the principles guiding his vision, in terms so general as to minimize the possibility for disagreement and allow widespread latitude for interpretation:

I believe America needs a government that is both smaller and more responsive. One that both works better and costs less. One that shifts authority from the federal level to states and localities as much as possible. One that relies upon entrepreneurs in the private sector when the private sector can do the job best. One that has fewer regulations and more incentives. One, in short, that has more common sense and seeks more common ground.[88]

Clinton continued to prioritize the economy, defining it as one of the government's essential responsibilities: "The federal government has another critical responsibility: creating the framework in which our economy can grow. By reducing the deficit, bringing interest rates down, holding inflation in check, restraining bad business practices, expanding opportunities for world trade, supporting research and technology, and increasing educational opportunity, the government plays a central role."[89] In defining government's economic role, Clinton retained more interventionist Democratic policies.

The final theme in Clinton's triad was community. Domestically, this translated into protecting the family, with the Family and Medical Leave Act a prominent symbolic victory; reducing television violence via the V-chip control system; and restoring racial harmony. Internationally, this translated into U.S. leadership in world affairs. Clinton again urged U.S. commitment to GATT and NAFTA, as well as the Summit of the Americas and the Asia Pacific Economic Council (APEC): "The global trend toward democracy and free markets is neither inevitable nor irreversible. Our well-being as a nation and our strength as a people depend upon maintaining our leadership abroad. America cannot lead by 'escaping,' retreating from our responsibilities or our commitments, or going our own way. Instead, we must lead and work with the community of nations."[90]

Repeatedly, when espousing the success of market-opening measures, Clinton would qualify his arguments by recognizing the transgressions of Japan and his administration's achievements in defending America's interests through forcing Japan to open its markets: "And we've negotiated twenty-one separate trade agreements, covering everything from computers to medical supplies. As a result, American exports to Japan have increased dramatically—by 85 percent in the sectors covered by the accords."[91] However, Clinton prioritized the political and security importance of the U.S. alliance with Japan over economic entanglements: "Our relationship with our partner in the Pacific, Japan, continues to deepen, despite occasional trade disagreements."[92]

President Clinton defined NAFTA and GATT as landmark measures in U.S. trade policy: "In this new era, we must never forget that the true measure of our people's security includes not only their physical safety, but their economic well-being, too. Decades from now, I believe people will look back at this period and see the most far-reaching changes in the world trading system in generations."[93]

President Clinton did not rhetorically emphasize the replacement of GATT by the World Trade Organization (WTO). The WTO was a stronger enforcement mechanism; while benefiting the United States in pressing other nations to open markets, it also contained possibilities for encroaching on U.S. domestic economic policies, causing decreased U.S. control. A reelection campaign, though, was no time for couching far-reaching and ultimately beneficial policy changes in a qualifying rhetoric. Clinton simply stated that these changes would benefit American workers and harked back to the optimistic rhetoric of the Reagan years:

This increasing international interdependence is seen by some as a threat to our nation and our values as Americans—but the truth is almost precisely the reverse. It is American values and principles—freedom, determination, market economies—that are ascendant around the globe. It is American companies that are gaining most from the rapid growth in international trade. It is American products made by American workers that are in highest demand as the standards of living improve in countries around the world.[94]

However, the controversy over the expansion of trade via multilateral trade pacts, which was perceived to be at the expense of American jobs, was not resolved. Downplayed by Clinton in the campaign, it was likely to be a second-term legislative battle, most specifically regarding reviewing fast track authority. Opposition to NAFTA led to the unlikely marriage of labor and Ralph Nader's Public Citizen interest group. In Public Citizen's "NAFTA's Three Year Reality," Nader charged NAFTA with the loss of 600,000 American jobs and increasing trade deficits with Japan and China. These arguments were fortified by the 1996 reports of these swelling deficits. The overall U.S. trade deficit reached an eight-year high of $114.2 billion. Sixty percent of this deterioration since 1993 was due to rising deficits with Mexico and Canada.[95] As plants closed, workers' testimonials reinforced these arguments. A worker laid off from a General Electric plant that had been shut down and moved to Mexico stated: "They put us out to pasture because we were making $15 hourly wages and they could get the work done in Mexico for 83 cents an hour."[96] The Clinton administration replied by blaming other nations' slow economic growth as responsible for the deficits. In addition, it cited the growth in export-related jobs and limited amount of worker-retraining claims as evidence of an improving trade situation. However, the admittedly small number of claims could easily be cited as a measure of the program's ineffectiveness or underutilization.

The election did not, however, hinge on the issue of trade pacts. Even Clinton's emphasis on the transition to the twenty-first century—with the inherent association with trade-related policies such as governmental reform and education—did not result in trade becoming a decisive voting issue. It did, however, remain a focal point for administration policy through Clinton's emphasis on improving competitiveness in an increasingly interdependent world.

PRELUDE TO A SECOND TERM

Having won a decisive reelection victory, Clinton continued the theme of transition, and hence the need for bold and decisive leadership, in his second inaugural address: "a moment that will define our course and our character for decades to come."[97] The grand themes inherent to an inaugural allowed Clinton to continue his campaign themes of opportunity, responsibility, and community: "The preeminent mission of our new Government is to give all Americans an opportunity, not a guarantee, but a real opportunity, to build better lives."[98] Clinton gave continued preeminence to international economic leadership in a changing world: "The world is no longer divided into two hostile camps. Instead, now we are building bonds with nations that once were our adversaries. Growing connections of commerce and culture give us a chance to lift the fortunes and spirits of people the world over."[99]

Domestically, Clinton continued to emphasize education: "In this new land, education will be every citizen's most prized possession."[100] Clinton's governing themes were consistent, and no more evident than in his 1997 State of the Union Address, establishing the direction of his second administration: "I come before you tonight with a challenge as great as any in our peacetime history and a plan of action to meet that challenge, to prepare our people for the bold new world of the 21st century."[101] Clinton continued to emphasize urgency in this time of transition: "The new promise of the global economy, the information age, unimagined new work, life-enhancing technology, all these are ours to seize. This is our honor and our challenge. We must be shapers of events, not observers. For if we do not act, the moment will pass, and we will lose the best possibilities of our future."[102]

In the absence of the Cold War, Clinton attempted to invent a new enemy to galvanize the citizenry into action: "We face no imminent threat, but we do have an enemy. The enemy of our time is inaction."[103] However, he failed to propose any bold new restructuring of government. While continuing with his themes of opportunity, responsibility, and community, he focused on limited, specific actions the government could take to ensure progress towards the twenty-first century. Not surprisingly, he named education as the number one goal and focused on national objectives: "Now, looking ahead, the greatest step of all, the high threshold of the future we must now cross, and my number one priority for the next 4 years is to ensure that all Americans have the best education in the world."[104]

Clinton devoted a significant portion of this speech to specific education goals, listing ten principles for action. All were at the national level, thus minimizing encroachment on state and local powers: national standards, teacher certification, improving literacy, early childhood education, public school choice, character education, structural improvements, universal college education, lifetime learning and retraining, and connection to the internet.[105] President Clinton explicitly defined education as important precisely because of its relation to competitiveness:

We must understand the significance of this endeavor: One of the greatest sources of our strength throughout the Cold War was a bipartisan foreign policy; because our future was at stake, politics stopped at the water's edge. Now I ask you and I ask all our Nation's Governors; I ask parents, teachers, and citizens all across America for a new non-partisan commitment to education because education is a critical national security issue for our future, and politics must stop at the schoolhouse door.[106]

In trade, Clinton reasserted his commitment to the global economy and to the expansion of trade and justified the Mexican loan. He referred to President Truman's international commitments at the beginning of the Cold War as remaining necessary to a world after the Cold War. He evoked President Kennedy's "thousand days" in reiterating the importance of immediate action. Most important, Clinton underscored the need for renewed vigor and commitment to international leadership to remain strong domestically.

CONCLUSION

President Clinton thus integrated domestic and foreign policy explicitly and consistently in his rhetoric on trade. His policy did not markedly differ from previous executives in expanding and supporting free trade. It was distinct, though, for both the emphasis Clinton placed on trade in his administration's agenda and for the active government role he supported.

If we assess Clinton's trade policy by the measure of the trade deficit, it would be an unmitigated failure, for the trade deficit increased every year of President Clinton's administration. If, however, assessment of Clinton's trade policy is measured by legislative accomplishments and policy changes, a markedly different picture emerges. Passage of NAFTA and GATT, the transition to the World Trade Organization, and, in effect, the continued expansion of free trade were all economic successes. Garnering support for related domestic changes in education, worker retraining, and a more interventionist government on economic issues were also indices of success.

Rhetorically, it is not surprising that President Clinton downplayed the deficit and highlighted the passage of NAFTA. Rhetorically, it is not surprising that Clinton deemphasized trade policy while emphasizing the related issues of education, strengthening the domestic economy, and restructuring government. Rhetorically, it is most significant that President Clinton emphasized the domestic impact of trade as an intermestic issue.

However, with the continuing public perception of trade transgressions by foreign nations and the popular assumption that NAFTA had cost American jobs, as had the continued trade deficit—especially the deficit with Japan and China—a limited presidential rhetoric addressed to select audiences was not effective in rebutting these arguments. Perhaps it had been effective in the past, when trade was not on the public agenda in any sustained manner, but it was no longer effective in an era when trade became an issue for public discussion.

Although President Clinton's rhetoric was notable for connecting the domestic and foreign implications of trade as an intermestic issue, the dilemma for presidential rhetoric on trade as an agenda item remains. The president still must balance popular economic nationalism with a growing interdependence—the increasing need to rely on multilateral institutions despite decreasing control and increasing likelihood of interference with domestic politics. Republican presidents still have an easier task of balancing party preferences with the executive preference for free trade. Democratic presidents, even centrists like Clinton, must continue to navigate between the executive preference for free trade and the traditional Democratic constituency preference for protectionist measures. Future presidents will face even greater dangers in balancing budget strictures, the trade deficit, and economic interdependence.

NOTES

1. All statements from the conference are taken from William J. Clinton, "Introduction," *President Clinton's New Beginning* (New York: Donald I. Fine, 1992), 3.

2. Pamela Fessler, "Clinton Announces Conference to Gauge Economic Options," *Congressional Quarterly*, 28 November 1992, 3709.

3. Clinton, *New Beginning*, 3–4.

4. Thomas L. Friedman, "Experts Gather for Conference on the Economy," *New York Times,* 14 December 1992, B6.

5. Michael Kelly, "Despite Some Signs of Recovery, Clinton Points to Economic Perils," *New York Times*, 10 November 1992, A20.

6. Ibid.

7. Friedman, "Experts Gather."

8. Ibid.

9. Kelly, "Signs of Recovery," A1.

10. Friedman, "Experts Gather."

11. Sylvia Nasar, "Some Voices Missing at Clinton's Conference," *New York Times*, 21 December 1992, D1.

12. Clinton, *New Beginning*, 61.

13. Ibid., 4.

14. Ibid., 356.

15. Thomas L. Friedman, "Professor-Elect on TV: More Than a Talk Show," *New York Times*, 15 December 1992, B11.

16. William J. Clinton, "Inaugural Address," *Public Papers of the Presidents of the United States* (Washington, D.C.: U.S. Government Printing Office, 20 January 1993), 1.

17. Ibid.

18. Michael Hirsh and Karen Breslau, "Closing the Deal," *Newsweek*, 6 March 1995, 34.

19. William J. Clinton, "Remarks at the American University Centennial Celebration," *Public Papers of the Presidents of the United States* (Washington, D.C.: U.S. Government Printing Office, 26 February 1993), 207.

20. Ibid.

21. Ibid., 208.

22. Ibid., 209–210.

23. Ibid., 210.

24. Ibid., 212.

25. Clinton was also late in his support for NAFTA due to his preoccupation with passage of the budget.

26. Bill Clinton, "Teleconference Remarks on NAFTA to the United States Chamber of Commerce," *Weekly Compilation of Presidential Documents* (hereafter cited as *WCPD*), 1 November 1993, 2226.

27. Ibid.

28. Ibid.

29. Bill Clinton, "Remarks on NAFTA to Employees of Lexmark International in Lexington," *WCPD,* 4 November 1993, 2261.

30. Bill Clinton, "Teleconference Remarks on NAFTA to Chamber of Commerce," 2226.

31. Ibid., 2227.

32. Ibid.

33. Ibid.

34. Bill Clinton, "Remarks on Endorsements of the North American Free Trade Agreement," *WCPD*, 2 November 1993, 2242.

35. Clinton, "Remarks on NAFTA to Employees of Lexmark International," 2258.

36. Bill Clinton, "Teleconference on NAFTA with Midwest Farmers, Ranchers, and Agricultural Broadcasters and an Exchange with Reporters," *WCPD*, 5 November 1993, 2275.

37. Clinton, "Teleconference Remarks on NAFTA to Chamber of Commerce," 2232.

38. Ibid., 2228.

39. Ibid.

40. Ibid.

41. Ibid.

42. Clinton, "Remarks on Endorsements," 2242.

43. Ibid.

44. Ibid., 2243.

45. Bill Clinton, "Remarks on Signing the Message Transmitting NAFTA Legislation to the Congress and an Exchange with Reporters," *WCPD*, 3 November 1993, 2245.

46. Ibid.

47. Patrick Worsnip, "Mounting Isolationist Tide a U.S. Policy Worry," *Pittsburgh Post-Gazette*, 23 January 1995, A5.

48. Michael Elliot, "Why the Mexican Crisis Matters," *Newsweek*, 13 February 1995, 29.

49. Ibid., 28.

50. Bill Clinton, "Remarks at the Edmund A. Walsh School of Foreign Service at Georgetown University," *WCPD,* 10 November 1994, 2350.

51. Ibid., 2354.

52. Ibid.

53. Bill Clinton, "Address before a Joint Session of the Congress on the State of the Union," *WCPD*, 24 January 1995, 97.

54. Ibid.

55. Ibid., 106.

56. Hirsh and Breslau, "Closing the Deal."

57. Bill Clinton, "Remarks to the United Auto Workers Convention," *WCPD*, 12 June 1995, 1046.

58. Ibid.

59. Ibid.

60. Ibid.

61. Bill Clinton, "Remarks to Employees of McDonnell Douglas in Long Beach, California," *WCPD*, 23 February 1993, 359.

62. The remaining four challenges were building stronger families, reducing crime, protecting the environment, and reinventing government.

63. Bill Clinton, "Remarks to the United States Agricultural Communicators Congress," *WCPD*, 16 July 1996, 1260.

64. Ibid.

65. Bill Clinton, "Remarks at the Dedication of the Nashville Wharf in New Orleans, Louisiana," *WCPD*, 18 March 1996, 525.

66. Bill Clinton and Al Gore, *Putting People First* (New York: Times Books, 1992). Bill Clinton, *Between Hope and History* (New York: Random House, 1997).

67. Clinton, *Between Hope and History*, xi–xii.

68. Ibid., 10.

69. Ibid., 11.

70. Ibid., 14.

71. Ibid., 14–15.

72. Ibid., 22.

73. Ibid., 25.

74. Ibid.

75. Ibid., 28.

76. Ibid., 29.

77. Ibid., 34.

78. Ibid., 34–35.

79. Ibid., 35.

80. Ibid., 36.

81. Ibid.

82. Ibid., 37.

83. Ibid., 41.

84. Ibid., 48.

85. Ibid., 43.

86. Ibid., 90.

87. Ibid.

88. Ibid., 91–92.

89. Ibid., 95.

90. Ibid., 145.

91. Ibid., 154.

92. Ibid., 153.

93. Ibid., 164–165.

94. Ibid., 167.

95. Martin Crutsinger, "Chile Seeks Place in NAFTA," *Pittsburgh Post-Gazette*, 24 February 1997, A3.

96. Ibid.

97. Bill Clinton, "Inaugural Address," *WCPD*, 20 January 1997, 60.

98. Ibid., 61.

99. Ibid., 62.

100. Ibid.

101. Bill Clinton, "Address before a Joint Session of the Congress on the State of the Union," *WCPD*, 4 February 1997, 136.

102. Ibid.

103. Ibid.

104. Ibid., 137.

105. Ibid., 138–139.

106. Ibid., 139–140.

Conclusion:
The Rhetoric of Intermestic Issues

A SUMMARY OF PRESIDENTIAL TRADE RHETORIC

Trade, which involves a blend of foreign and domestic policy, is the classic intermestic issue. In the history of presidential arguments on trade, the weight given each side of the equation has varied with both the occupants of the office and the historical circumstances, yet the arguments themselves have remained remarkably static.

Trade legislation has always been the centerpiece for trade rhetoric. However, the institutional structure for legislation has shifted from domestic politics, when tariffs were the main source of government revenue, to unilateral pacts, including the Trade and Tariff Act of 1934 and the Trade Expansion Act of 1961; and then to bilateral, and, now, multilateral, pacts, such as NAFTA, GATT, and the World Trade Organization (WTO).

In times of transition, trade has received greater presidential emphasis. In establishing the government, the founding fathers requested guidance in Hamilton's *Report on Manufacturers*. Similarly, the Compromise of 1833 forestalled the Civil War. In the 1880s, the issue became one of forced reciprocity: this was an argument that would remain potent, resonating with economic nationalism. In the aftermath of the Great Depression, Franklin Roosevelt was responsible for one of the most significant changes in trade policy: shifting the emphasis in trade from domestic politics to an export-oriented foreign policy.

In addition to circumstances, the preferences of individual presidents have also greatly influenced trade policy. While all contemporary presidents have favored free trade, the extent to which they have prioritized trade policy has varied. Presidents Kennedy and Nixon used trade policy as a tool of foreign policy. President Carter ignored trade, instead giving priority to human rights on his foreign policy agenda. Presidents Reagan and Bush, while asserting U.S. interests in advocating fair trade, treated trade policy as a necessary hindrance. If we examine President Clinton from the perspective of both circumstances and individual preference, he has given trade a domestic emphasis by defining it as essential to economic strength. He has not, however, made it a prominent agenda item. Similar to Reagan and Bush, he has made a concerted and public push for trade legislation only when forced to by circumstances.

Perhaps the greatest lessons can be learned from examining the rhetoric of Presidents Reagan, Bush and Clinton. There are ideological contrasts between these Republican and Democratic presidents: between a president rhetorically disallowing intervention in the economy while allowing a dramatic reversal in policy; a president focused on foreign policy and treating trade as such; and a president intent on domestic policy, willing to intervene in the economy, continuing the push for a major trade pact, and yet minimizing the foreign policy implications of trade.

Despite these different priorities, Presidents Reagan, Bush, and Clinton all kept trade off the public agenda, except when necessitated by circumstances. All failed to recognize the potential of yearly international economic summits. Instead, they accepted the vagaries of the forum's pronouncements and continued the empty ritualistic nature of the meetings. Future presidents would do better to capitalize on the publicity of these summits and use them both as a forum for U.S. leadership in international economic affairs and as a medium for defending U.S. trading interests.

In addition, Presidents Reagan, Bush, and Clinton acted unilaterally, bilaterally, and multilaterally in trade policy. The public, however, seems most satisfied when the United States acts aggressively, and thus unilaterally, to defend domestic interests. Thus, the issue remains how to activate the free trade–oriented public without arousing the protectionist public. Can economics be handled aggressively without reverting to economic nationalism? As Presidents Bush and Clinton defined America's next battleground as economic, they provoked such antagonism.

Most critically, is economics an effective primary motivator in foreign policy? How can a president promote a vision of American leadership in the economic realm? Presidents Reagan, Bush, and Clinton all recognized the need to fight a new surge of isolationism, both economic and military. This was heightened in Bush and Clinton's presidencies in the post–Cold

War era. All three presidents chose to emphasize America's continued ability to compete given fair trade, harking back to the spirit and optimism of the American dream as an economic land of opportunity.

A closer examination of Presidents Bush and Clinton and their vision of trade in a post–Cold War world reveals a distinct difference in the manner in which both presidents worked with Congress on intermestic issues. Bush chose to portray Congress as the enemy and as responsible for the recession. Clinton was, especially after the midterm elections, dealing with an opposition Congress, which he nonetheless needed to achieve bipartisan support for trade legislation. Both presidents altered their economic rhetoric due to election year pressures. Bush, anticipating problems, finally began to address the domestic economy. Clinton, following midterm results, embraced a new theme—the "New Covenant"—which rhetorically minimized the amount of government activism without changing his conception of economic policy.

President Clinton's most dramatic departure from President Bush was precisely his focus on the economy. Clinton explicitly integrated the domestic and foreign policy elements of the economy. While his administration's first priority was the recovery of the domestic economy, Clinton also emphasized global change and its implications for the global economy.

In summary, President Bush neglected trade both politically and rhetorically. He reacted to international events and failed to integrate international economics with domestic plans despite eventually adopting an intermestic rhetoric. President Clinton captured the essence of trade as a foreign and domestic policy issue from the outset and placed trade high on his agenda, yet he failed to present a comprehensive approach to trade as his administration pieced together unilateral, bilateral, and multilateral actions. During Clinton's first term, the trade deficit increased, whereas during Bush's administration, it had decreased. The decrease in the trade deficit during Bush's administration did not seem to affect the public's perception of a weak economy, which was grounded in the reality of the continued domestic recession. Similarly, the increase in the trade deficit during President Clinton's administration did not seem to affect the public's perception of a recovering, healthy economy. In both cases, the trade deficit, which was reported routinely, was nonetheless difficult to rhetorically translate into concrete economic effects.

If the trade deficit does not automatically impinge on the public's perception of the state of the economy, what is its significance in terms of policy and rhetoric and as an intermestic issue? Trade policy is an easy scapegoat in times of economic crisis, as well as in less problematic situations, such as when domestic industry–specific jobs are lost. Presidents miss a critical opportunity for managing protectionist pressures by failing to take advantage of the persuasive possibilities of trade. More important, clinging to an unexamined rhetoric based on the free trade paradigm unnecessarily restricts and hinders trade policy.

RHETORICAL STRATEGIES FOR INTERMESTIC ISSUES

The president cannot inflame protectionist pressures via economic nationalism while promoting a rhetoric of cooperation via multilateral and bilateral trade agreements. It is imperative that the executive protect American trading interests and aggressively promote actions in defense of free but fair trade. The United States must reconcile its new role as economic leader with the nature of multilateral institutions and agreements. While America's economic leadership role is evolving, there is a vital need for a clearer and more consistent presidential rhetoric asserting U.S. goals while protecting U.S. interests.

The free market paradigm impinges on American economic power. While serving as a congressional representative, current Republican Governor of Pennsylvania Tom Ridge stated: "The rhetoric of free trade has been an impediment to the development of a comprehensive, responsive trade policy. It has been an encumbrance, and to those who have lost their jobs because of blind subservience to it, it has been a curse. Free trade has proven to be very expensive and continual reliance is pure folly."[1]

The free market may remain an economic ideal. The free market paradigm, however, should not unnecessarily constrain trade policy. The continuing reliance on the principle of free, but fair, trade in presidential rhetoric illustrates the false dichotomy between fair trade and protectionism. The president needs to rhetorically highlight, and therefore politically strengthen, programs to assist displaced workers and domestic industries.[2] This can be done without resorting to a misguided protectionism. With the growing importance of economic interdependence, the breakdown of the paradigm of the Cold War, and the ensuing combination of political security and economic interdependence, presidents must adjust their rhetorical arguments to the political realities of trade.

The great dilemma in presidential rhetoric on trade remains. As economic interdependence increases and competitiveness becomes even more vital to domestic economic strength, the problem is heightened by the perception of trade transgressions. Rhetorically, the president must balance demands for fair trade with efforts to minimize economic nationalism provoked by this rhetoric. The arcane details of trade policy, the continuing pervasiveness of nontariff barriers, and the impending negotiation of international trade agreements combine to make presidential leadership critical.

The rhetoric of previous presidents and the policy constraints and opportunities of trade as an intermestic issue suggest clear guidelines for presidential rhetoric in the domestic and foreign policy realms.

Prioritize Domestic Interests

First, presidents must prioritize domestic interests. If they are not seen as defending America's best interests, the trade transgressions of foreign nations may nullify the effectiveness of trade pacts. At its base, without a strong domestic economy, economic nationalism and isolationism will peak, as evidenced by the success of demagogic trade rhetoric in presidential primaries and in lower-level congressional rhetoric.

Maintain Consistency

Second, presidents must remain consistent despite the inconsistency of trade rhetoric. Most important, they must reconcile free trade with protectionist actions. This is most readily accomplished through a rhetoric stressing fair trade. In addition, presidents can address select audiences affected by trade. In doing so, they can acknowledge the existence of unfair trade, reconcile select protectionist actions without promoting them to prominent national agenda items, and convey an aura of action without publicly betraying a rhetoric of free trade.

Emphasize Institutional Legitimacy

Nonetheless, the national interest and, thus, the executive's prerogative remain with the economic principle of free trade. Presidents must therefore rely on institutional legitimacy though emphasizing executive wisdom, the national interest, and historical precedent. In addition, they must reconcile unilateral, bilateral, and multilateral trading pacts. The arcane nature of trade agreements and policy lends itself to minimizing contradictions. At the same time, this very same complexity allows simplification in promoting economic nationalism.

Promote Economic Competitiveness

The first three strategies—prioritizing domestic interests, maintaining consistency, and emphasizing institutional legitimacy—are essential if the president is to be able to make the policy changes necessary in meeting the demands of increased economic competitiveness.

The politics and rhetoric of the nation-state must make allowances for the economic realities of interdependence. This is not to say that nations should not protect their own economic interests, but rather that the grounding of economic rhetoric in outdated assumptions of the market does not allow for adapting to interdependence. A trade deficit is not necessarily the result of unfair trade, as foreign production and investment can contribute to a strong economy. Though protection of a manufacturing base is essential to the U.S. economy, the rhetorical disallowance of an economic shift away from a manufacturing based economy will impede the necessary political reallocation of resources and amount to an economic calamity.

SUMMARY

In the 1990s and beyond, the executive coordination of an aggressive trade offensive is necessary. Such an offensive can only be made acceptable through changing the terms of debate, which will require an active public campaign by the president. Historically it has been proven wise for presidents to avoid activating a latently protectionist public, as if they continue to minimize actions taken in the name of fair trade and the trade deficit persists, protectionist pressures will not abate and workers in dying industries will remain a political liability. Thus, the traditional strategies for success in presidential rhetoric on trade—remaining reactive and preaching the virtues of free trade—are no longer predictors of success and, in fact, are more likely to trigger economic decline.

The terms of debate for the executive should not be those of free trade, fair trade, or protection. Presidents must reconcile the economic circumstances of an interdependent world (resulting in managed trade, whether publicly acknowledged or not) with the traditional political philosophies prohibiting intervention in the market. Moreover, they must reconcile nationalistic tendencies in trade, including the unnecessary protection of domestic industries and fear of foreign investment, with the realities of an interdependent world economy. The nature of intermestic issues demands presidential leadership in reconciling domestic and foreign trade issues.

NOTES

1. Thomas J. Ridge, "Should Congress Adopt the House-Passed 'Gephardt Amendment'?" *Congressional Digest*, June–July 1987, 180.

2. For a discussion of the need to strengthen domestic trade policies, see Alfred Eckes, "Trading American Interests," *Foreign Affairs*, 71, no. 4 (Fall 1992): 135–154.

Selected Bibliography

BOOKS

Amacher, Ryan C., Haberler, Gottfried, and Willett, Thomas D. *Challenges to a Liberal International Economic Order.* Washington, D.C.: American Enterprise Institute, 1979.

Bauer, Raymond, de Sola Pool, Ithiel, and Dexter, Lewis Anthony. *American Business and Public Policy.* Chicago: Aldine-Atherton, 1972.

Blumenthal, Sidney. *Pledging Allegiance.* New York: HarperCollins, 1990.

Cohen, Stephen D. *The Making of United States Economic Policy.* 2nd ed. New York: Praeger, 1981.

Destler, I. M. *American Trade Politics.* Washington, D.C.: Institute for International Economics and the Twentieth Century Fund, 1986.

Dobson, John M. *Two Centuries of Tariffs.* Washington, D.C.: United States International Trade Commission, 1976.

Evans, John W. *The Kennedy Round in American Trade Policy.* Cambridge, MA: Harvard University Press, 1971.

Hamilton, Alexander, Jay, John, and Madison, James. *The Federalist.* Reprint. New York: Heritage Press, 1945.

House Miscellaneous Document no. 210, 53rd Cong., 2nd sess. In *Compilation of the Messages and Papers of the Presidents, 1789–1897.* Ed. J. D. Richardson. Vol. 4. Washington, D.C.: U.S. Government Printing Office, 1910.

Kernell, Samuel. *Going Public: New Strategies of Presidential Leadership.* Washington, D.C.: Congressional Quarterly Press, 1986.

Magaziner, Ira C., and Reich, Robert. *Minding America's Business.* New York: Vantage Books, 1983.

Metzger, Stanley D. *Trade Agreements and the Kennedy Round*. Fairfax, VA: Corner Publications, 1964.

Olson, Mancur. *The Rise and Decline of Nations*. New Haven, CT: Yale University Press, 1982.

Pastor, Robert. *Congress and the Politics of U.S. Foreign Economic Policy 1929–1976*. Berkeley: University of California Press, 1980.

Reich, Robert. *Tales of a New America*. New York: Random House, 1987.

————. *The Next American Frontier*. New York: Penguin Books, 1984.

Schick, Allen. *Making Economic Policy in Congress*. Washington, D.C.: American Enterprise Institute, 1983.

Stanwood, Edward. *American Tariff Controversies in the Nineteenth Century*. 1st ed., 2 vols. New York: Russell and Russell, 1903.

Taussig, F. W. *State Papers and Speeches on the Tariff*. Clifton, NJ: Augustus M. Kelley Publishers, 1972.

————. *The Tariff History of the United States*. 7th ed. New York: G. P. Putnam's Sons, 1923.

————. *Some Aspects of the Tariff Question*. Vol. 7 of *Harvard Economic Studies*. Cambridge, MA: Harvard University Press, 1915.

ARTICLES

Barilleaux, Ryan J. "The President, 'Intermestic Issues,' and the Risks of Policy Leadership." *Presidential Studies Quarterly*, 15, no. 4 (Fall 1985): 754–767.

Ceaser, James W., Thurow, Glenn E., Tulis, Jeffrey, and Bessette, Joseph M. "The Rise of the Rhetorical Presidency." *Presidential Studies Quarterly*, 11, no. 2 (Spring 1981): 158–171.

Dapstein, Ethan B. "Workers and the World Economy." *Foreign Affairs*, 75, no. 4 (May/June 1996): 16–37.

Eckes, Alfred. "Trading American Interests." *Foreign Affairs*, 71, no. 4 (Fall 1992): 135–154.

Harrison, Selig S., and Prestowitz, Clyde V., Jr. "Pacific Agenda: Defense or Economics?" *Foreign Policy*, 79 (Summer 1990): 56–76.

Hormats, Robert D. "The Presidency in the High Competition, Hi-Tech Eighties." *Presidential Studies Quarterly*, 13 (Spring 1983): 255–260.

Marvel, Howard P., and Ray, Edward J. "The Kennedy Round: Evidence on the Regulation of International Trade in the United States." *American Economic Review*, 73 (March 1983): 190–197.

Wander, Philip. "The Rhetoric of American Foreign Policy." *Quarterly Journal of Speech*, 70, no. 4 (November 1984): 339–361.

Windt, Theodore. "Presidential Rhetoric: Definition of a Discipline of Study." In *Essays in Presidential Rhetoric*, ed. Theodore Windt and Beth Ingold. 2nd ed. Dubuque, IA: Kendall/Hunt Publishing Company, 1987.

Index

About the Author

DELIA B. CONTI is Assistant Professor in Speech Communication at Penn State University, McKeesport. Her research interests and earlier writings have been in presidential rhetoric, political communications, and women's studies.

ISBN 0-275-96109-5

90000>

EAN

9 780275 961091

HARDCOVER BAR CODE